C000094317

 guide

LondonbyLondon

The
insiders'
guide

LondonbyLondon

Edited by Paul Carr and Clare Christian

FRIDAY

All opinions expressed in this book are the contributors' own and not those of the editors or Friday Book Publishing.

First published in Great Britain in 2004 by
Friday Book Publishing Ltd
PO Box 608, Haywards Heath, RH16 1HX

www.fridaybooks.co.uk

British Library Cataloguing in Publication Data

A catalogue record for this book is available from the British Library

Illustrations by Andrew Clare

ISBN 0-9548318-0-2

Design by Staziker Jones
www.stazikerjones.co.uk

Printed and bound in Great Britain by MWL Print Group
www.mwl.co.uk

Contents

Welcome to London by London

You find no man, at all intellectual, who is willing to leave London. No, Sir, when a man is tired of London, he is tired of life; for there is in London all that life can afford.

Samuel Johnson

London, that great cesspool into which all the loungers and idlers of the Empire are irresistibly drained.

Sir Arthur Conan Doyle – *A Study in Scarlet*

Ah, London. Londinium. The Great Wen. You don't have to be an idle intellectual lounger to live here, but it helps. It also helps to have a good tolerance for alcohol, no real sense of smell and a friendly guide that will explain the city's quirks without scoffing at your ignorance or trying to steal your wallet. London by London is that guide.

The London by London community began two years ago when a group of Londoners began sending out a weekly email of questions and observations about the capital.

The first issue was sent to ten people, who were encouraged to reply to the questions and to post their own.

Word of the email quickly began to spread and by the end of the first month over 500 people had signed up to be 'LBLers'. After six months, the subscriber total had passed the 10,000 mark.

Since those humble beginnings, the LBL community has discussed and debated almost every aspect of London, its places and its people. From the shape of the road bollards around King's Cross, to the name of the Oxford Street evangelist, to the best place in the capital to buy mint choc chip ice cream – you name it, we've discussed it. In fact, if there's a snippet of information about London that hasn't been shared by London by Londoners then frankly, it's probably not worth sharing.

Which brings us to the book you are holding in your hands. In these 250-plus pages, you will find a lovingly compiled selection of LBL wisdom and wit from our first two years. It represents the collected knowledge of hundreds of Londoners on hundreds of subjects – from that ice cream question to details of London's secret underground newsagent. And just about everything in between.

Read it carefully, learn its secrets, join the community and, most importantly, tell us what you know.

The idle intellectual loungers of London thank you.

London by London

Join the London by London community!
Sign up for the free weekly email at
www.londonbylondon.co.uk

Observations

Look around you. What do you see? A mysterious queue of people on the Aldwych. A man being followed by a crow. Some odd shaped bollards. But what are they doing there? And what's that sound? An air raid siren? In the middle of London? Surely not.

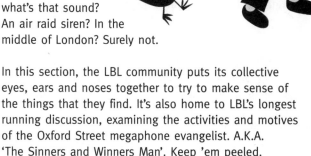

In this section, the LBL community puts its collective eyes, ears and noses together to try to make sense of the things that they find. It's also home to LBL's longest running discussion, examining the activities and motives of the Oxford Street megaphone evangelist. A.K.A. 'The Sinners and Winners Man'. Keep 'em peeled.

Sounds and smells

BOMB

On Sunday morning at 10am, I woke to the sound of an air-raid siren. It went on until 11am. I live in Clapham and it sounded quite distant, but was clearly audible and sounded like a classic war film.

Is this normal? Should I have heard this before and just not been awake early enough? Is it some wide-boy with a really annoying car alarm and if so, why didn't his neighbours sort it out in under an hour?

🗩 **Maybeitisallinmyhead**

I live in Battersea and also heard the air-raid siren. I found out that it goes off when there is a gas leak from one of the Gasometers situated on the Chelsea Bridge side of Battersea Park. To hear it from Clapham is mighty impressive though!

🗩 **Mario**

I was woken up by the same siren – it dragged me out of bed at a friend's in Battersea with a massive World Cup-induced hangover. We were wondering whether it was a four-minute warning, whether we should shelter under tables, wrap wet towels round our heads, etc. But nothing happened.

However when my friend gave me a lift home traffic was gridlocked. We found out that there had been a gas leak from some gas works or gasholder or something in Battersea, and that had set off the siren. They had closed roads, evacuated houses, and so on. It was all over the local news.

🗩 **Stuart**

ALARM

I work in a lab in Cleveland Street W1 and get in fairly early. At around 8am I always hear a siren/ alarm that doesn't sound like any other I've heard. It's two-tone, kinda hollow and echoey. It goes off for around three to four seconds many times over a period of about 15 minutes. Does anyone know what it is?

💬 **Flameboy**

The strange noise around the Cleveland Street area could well be the sound of some hapless student trying to nick a book from the University of Westminster's library. I used to attend this fine seat of learning and I heard a similar sounding alarm go off many many times in my undergraduate days while studying in the Riding House Street site. It might be coming from the library in the New Cavendish Street site but I'm pretty sure that Westminster Uni security systems are the source. Hope this helps.

💬 **PRguru Josh**

I work just round the corner from Cleveland Street and often hear that alarm. I used to work in Sloane Square and on my walk from South Kensington tube in the mornings I used to hear exactly the same alarm round there too. I guess it's some generic fire/evacuation alarm being tested but it's not my building's because ours sounds like the opening bars of Ash's 'Burn Baby Burn'.

💬 **goldsoundz**

SMELL

I've been living in and around Rotherhithe/Surrey Quays for the last three years. Every now and then the air is filled with a sort of sweet plastic/chemical smell. It's a very distinct smell and it's all over the area but I have only ever smelled it around Docklands. I was on the Isle of Dogs the other day and it was there too.

Presumably it's some factory process? Are we all being slowly poisoned by a secret government-funded anti-Eastender project? Can anyone satisfy my olfactory curiosity?

💬 **Jonny**

Has anyone else noticed that weird sulphur/stink bomb/fart smell at the bottom of the final escalator, as you exit the underground from the Jubilee line at Waterloo? I have never noticed it in the mornings – only in the evenings at around 6–7pm. What is it, where it is coming from and why don't they eliminate it?

💬 **Snowbeetle**

I live on the Isle Of Dogs and every time the wind comes from over the Thames from Greenwich, we get a yucky wheaty smell. I was told that the smell comes from a factory near the southern entrance to the Blackwall Tunnel on the Greenwich Peninsula that makes dry dog food.

I have heard from 'islanders' who have been here since before the property boom that the smell used to be really quite awful until recent times, when the factory tidied up their act a bit. I understand it was the result of some sort of pollution directive.

💬 **Oz**

I grew up in Kent, and some of my earlier journeys to London were to White Hart Lane to see Spurs get beaten by my team (who I won't name for fear of abuse). My travels took me past Canary Wharf at which point I always noticed what I would describe as an horrific smell, but in line with the sweet plastic/chemical smell you describe.

I was told that it came from the sugar factory based there. Hard to believe that such a product would produce so horrible a smell, but there you go.

💬 **Smalldelapaul**

When I lived in Willesden a couple of years ago, the local paper carried a story about a woman who had witnessed a miracle – her toast had come out of the toaster with a cross on it. It was illustrated by a picture of the woman with this wondrous piece of toast, eerily backlit (obviously the journalist holding a torch from below) and the headline 'Father, Son and the Holy Toast'.

Local papers are tops.

💬 **Woody**

I'm guessing the chemical smell you have discovered is Westferry printing works, on the banks of Mill Quay on the Isle of Dogs. I used to live across the water from it and also up-wind. Seems the most likely culprit aside from a passing toxic barge.

💬 **Anonymous**

People watching

NOW WASH YOUR HANDS

I just thought I'd canvass some general opinion (and have a bit of a rant) on the subject of toilet 'attendants' in poncey bars/clubs. Why are they there?! Someone told me that they 'rent' the space in the loos and have to make their money back somehow, by supplying us with perfumes/deodorants/hair spray/lollipops (why lollipops?) etc., but, if this is true (anyone know?), why would anyone rent toilet space in the first place? It just baffles me. And there's no way I'm paying someone for a squirt of soap and a paper handtowel – I'm perfectly capable of using the soap dispenser by myself, thank you very much, and using soap and handtowels is a basic requirement after I've used the facilities, not an 'added extra'. They're just annoying!

Am I shouting into the darkness here, or is anyone else with me on this? When, why and how did this start, and why are they allowed to be there? And it's only at weekends, not every night. Do they think that people lose the faculty to wash their hands without assistance once the weekend rolls around?!

In bafflement and the hope that I'm not alone.

💬 PeeGee

You are not alone PeeGee. I can't understand why those 'attendants' are there either.

Not only do I not understand why they are there, but I do not like them. They are really intimidating (well the ones in the ladies loos are). They sit there staring at you like you're invading their privacy in the privvy and I've never yet felt able to help myself to the array of toiletries on offer because I just want to get out before they start having a go. I don't care if my skirt is tucked into my knickers, I just have to escape sharpish after a cursory hand-drying effort and a coin left in their saucer.

Hmmm perhaps that's why they're there? To speed things up a bit? The queues in the ladies on the weekend can be a bit slow. Still don't like them though.

💬 **mappeal**

Yes I quite agree that these washroom 'attendants' are annoying. I have a journalist friend who tried to write an article about them, but apparently since they don't receive minimum wage they're technically illegal, so the bars deny all knowledge of them, and none of the attendants would give an interview. It all seems very unofficial. I think they would be less annoying if they were just selling useful things like mints, condoms, poems, chat up lines, emergency exits and copies of LBL. I don't like the soap on my hands thing – it makes me feel like I ought to be obliged to give them a tip.

💬 **No, I Don't Need You To Hold My Willy While I Pee**

PeeGee, I think you may have opened a real hornet's nest here. I couldn't agree more with what you say – on the whole, these guys are a waste of space. There are those who sit back and offer you towels/aftershave etc., only if they are asked, and are good for an inebriated chat. But they're a tiny minority, unfortunately – the annoying, hard-selling twat is by far the norm.

Ever since my brother got slung out of my 30th party for not succumbing to their faux-pally, in-your-face ways (OK he was 'powdering his nose' but then so was everyone else at the party), I take great pleasure in stonewalling these parasites, going straight past them to the hand dryer. And if, as some places do, they've disabled the dryer, I'll walk out with wet hands (after giving them a vigorous shake over the pile of hand towels of course). Try it – it's very cathartic.

💬 **SFULG**

I'm right with you PeeGee. Toilet Monkeys are a scourge on our fair city. The last thing I want is an ugly muppet staring at me while I piss. What on earth do they get out of it? Standing in a toilet all night, with that stench all around them, people passing by all the time palpably having a much better time than they are. It seems, though, that the capital may be taking this on board. I've noticed something of a reduction in Toilet Monkey numbers over the last few months – *The Living Room* in Islington seems to have dispensed with theirs for instance, and, with any luck, we may be moving towards extinction in the not-too-distant. Like those stupid dress codes that every bar seemed to have a couple of years back. I haven't been turned away from a bar for my jeans and trainers in ages.

💬 **Sudonim**

Yeah, they get on my nerves too. I got really cross with myself one evening because I kept giving this woman a quid every time I went to the loo, just because she was there. I reckon that by the time one has had a few bevvies, somebody giving you a lollipop (I agree, what is the point in that?), seems very kind and you just feel obliged to pay one whole pound for it. I'm stupid, I know, it's all part of Rip-Off Britain. Having travelled in the US, the obligation to pay a 15 to 20 per cent tip there seems outrageous at first, but at least you get some value-added service for your dosh. And once you have tipped, they fall over themselves to please.

💬 **Missing London**

The point of toilet valets/attendents is two-fold:
1) to prevent the mindless vandalism in our toilets which costs us a lot of money and also puts you the customer out when you can't use the facility; and
2) to keep an eye out for drug use and other dodgy goings on.

The venue will normally book the valets depending on level of business so you can expect to see them on busy nights and less so during the week; however in the Westminster district it is now possible that it is a condition of the licence that valets must be present whenever the venue is open.

It is dependent on the venue but most of them will pay a nominal amount to have the toilets staffed and the valets rely on tips to make up their wages.

💬 **ClubManager**

The presence of those so-called toilet 'attendants' has riled me for some years now. They used to pop up in slightly poncier bars but now I see their useful work has spread to gig venues such as the *Forum* and *Astoria* (any night of the week, it's not just weekends).

It is not just that they chase you round the sinks armed with some foul-smelling blue liquid, but many of them seem to have a pretty aggressive attitude when you don't cough up for their 'services'.

💬 **Bib**

Calm down. Apparently they're primarily there to (try to) dissuade customers from nipping into the bogs together for a crafty line or five. Judging by the number of egocentric loud-mouthed braying sniffy Nathans in London bars nowadays it doesn't seem to be a very effective policy.

💬 Gradvalax

KING OF THE SWINGERS?

I work in an office at the top end of Great Portland Street and on an almost daily basis I hear strange noises that I can't explain. I'm sure they all come from the same source and every time I hear these noises I dash to the window but can never see anything.

I usually hear horse noises but by far the best is Tarzan's call to the beasts of the jungle. Every time I hear him I look out expectantly but fail to catch a glimpse of the jungle swinger!

Does anyone else hear these or other strange noises or possibly know where they come from? I'm sure Tarzan didn't escape from the zoo just to prance and yell around W1.

💬 The Jungle Warrior

The horse/tarzan noises you heard might be related to a strange man that I saw opposite Angel tube. He appears to own a motorbike and a sound effects machine, and one week whenever I was walking past (about three times in a day) he activated the sounds then proceeded to laugh manically at any passers-by who found his behaviour odd. Despite obviously doing this all day he didn't seem to grow tired of it. I saw him with the same crazed glint in his eye three days in a row, then he disappeared...

💬 Miles

The horse/tarzan noises puzzling Jungle Warrior occur round Farringdon too. I found out the source of this racket while on the pedestrian crossing on Rosebury Avenue, when a bloke came up behind me on a motorbike fitted with a *Dukes of Hazzard* style airhorn, and set it off with the sole purpose of scaring the living shit out of me.

It worked.

🖵 John

Does anyone else unfortunate enough to have to use London Bridge station every day remember the writing on the low wall on your left as you pull out of the station in a South Easterly direction that said 'Get to work you losers'?. Made me smile every time, like the loser I am.

🖵 Loser

The airhorn does both noises on a kind of loop, and the reason Jungle Warrior hasn't seen him is that he presumably shoots off straight afterwards on the bike. Is this legal? Does anyone know this man, and his reasons for being, well, a bit annoying?

🖵 Fulcanelli

You'll be thrilled to hear that his musical horn also does a convincing police siren, air-raid klaxon and high pitched squeak (similar to the noise the new single-decker buses insist on making to each other – but that's another story).

If you need further proof of the source of the Tarzan call, the courier in question can often be seen hanging around with his other courier chums of a weekday morning on Clerkenwell Road opposite St John's Gate by the *Texaco*. I'm convinced they spend most of the day just hanging out listening to his horn and laughing merrily as he regales them with his incredible tales of comedy horn-related capers.

If you do seek out this mobile comedy leviathan courier with his fascinating musical horn please let us all know if he makes a Tarzan-like noise as you shove the horn up his arse.

🗨 **Katanajim**

Just as I was reading about the various Tarzan sightings around London, what do I hear outside my office window in Brixton? None other than the king of the jungle himself in full cry. Spooky. Shame I got to the window too late to catch a glimpse though.

🗨 **Richsaint**

So just caught up with the courier with all of the noises on his bike. Very odd conversation ensued when I accosted him in front of our offices. Firstly he is wearing a suit and wrap around shades, not your usual leathers and scary tinted helmets. His name is Daudi (pronounced Daddy) and he works for a courier firm in Wimbledon.
When asked 'What's with the noises?' he fell back on that old favourite response, 'Because it makes me look very cool!'

And with that he jumped on his very old bike, gave us a couple of wolf whistles, and drove off to Oxford Street. Knob.

🗨 **Patrick**

NOT FORGETTING

If you're going to plot sightings of the Tarzan Horn Man, how about including the 'Sinners and Winners' man with the loudspeaker who we hear every day on Oxford Street? He's also been spotted on a Saturday by one of my colleagues at Waterloo station.

🗨 **Lizzie**

The admirably dedicated Scouse evangelist on Oxford Street. can also be heard at various London music events, seemingly harbouring a particular prejudice against festival-goers. At the last *Essential* festival he took to haranguing the circular queue for the free buses – when a couple of wags decided simply to follow him all the around the circle, pulling faces and giggling. Some distinctly un-Christian kicking ensued.

Also, a mate of mine, slightly the worse for wear one morning, told him to fuck off, at which point he explained that whilst a servant of God, he wasn't averse to giving profane unbelievers a good kicking. I'm presuming this irritating individual is a freelancer – anyone know if any particular group is unlucky enough to have him as a member?

🗨 **Tim**

We first saw the Sinners and Winners man at Notting Hill carnival last year – looks like he doesn't even take bank holidays off.

🗨 **Ni**

I went to Liverpool for the weekend a while back, and guess who was standing in Clayton Square with his effing megaphone? Yep!

🗨 **Dave**

The evangelicalist fundamentalist scouser once let rip into a megaphone about four inches from my ear, just by Selfridges. As I'm an opera singer my aural health is crucial to my living, so I lifted my music folder between my head and his instrument of torture. This earned me roaring chastisement as 'spawn of Satan', no less, which as a gay, liberal, Anglo-Catholic I consider a compliment from his ilk. But if anyone has a water pistol...

💬 **Maxbiker**

I first encountered the Sinners and Winners Scouse preacher man on the Northern line about a year ago. He was walking along asking people if they 'were believers' and when they said 'No' or ignored him he told them they were going to hell. I am a Christian, so when he asked me if I was a believer I said, 'Yes', and told him that I didn't think he had the right to tell people they were going to hell.

He proceeded to tell me that I was evil and that the devil was in me etc. I asked him how he knew that seeing as he didn't know me at all and we had only exchanged a few brief words. 'God's told me', he answered. (Great answer.) He went on to tell me how the Pope, the Queen and the Archbishop of Canterbury are all going to hell. I asked him who was going to heaven then... just him? God's chosen messenger? I never found out his answer, because as the doors opened at the next tube stop, he ran down the carriage and away. I confess to having shouted 'wanker' at him as he jumped off the train. Slapped wrists there. And that's his problem – he knows nothing about Christianity, or at least if he does, he preaches and practises little of it. It's people like him who give the majority of perfectly normal Christians a bad name.

What we need is a 6'5" body-building priest with a megaphone. That way, they can actually have a serious debate with no chance of him being able to kick back. I'd watch it.

💬 **Dr Bone**

The religious zealot that has been mentioned a fair bit recently used to stand in the tunnels of South Kensington tube station complete with megaphone and annoying attitude. Eventually he would leave, but it usually took the intervention of the British Transport Police. He can become quite violent when challenged.

One amusing incident stands out in my mind from last summer. One of the Revenue Protection staff went over to him and asked him to leave. He refused and stood his ground. The RPI again asked him to leave and the conversation became quite loud and heated. The nut then starts throwing his arms around wildly announcing that he preaches for God. The RPI replied 'I'm sure you do sir, but I box four times a week, now fuck off'. He did.

💬 **Jon**

How many years has it been since the London telephone codes changed from 0181/0171 to 020 8 or 020 7? Ages!

So why do so many numbnuts that both live and work in London still write 020 7XXX XXXX instead of the correct 020 7XXX XXXX? Does this wind anybody else up? Why do people still do it? Ignorance?

💬 **Gruncher**

Lost and found

FOUND

Does anyone have any idea how you'd go about tracking down a bag that you left in a cab when you don't know which company it was? The cab picked us up outside London Bridge station and took us to Bricklayer's Roundabout. And yes, I was hammered. I've tried phoning about 30 companies in the area but to no avail. Any ideas? I'm fresh out of them.

💬 Tiddle

It is always worth contacting the station lost property office. I was once out with my sister and don't even remember getting home, but she left her bag in the cab and a very thoughtful driver kindly drove back to the hotel he collected us from and returned the bag to reception who then rang her work (got the number from her mobile phone). Unfortunately he chose to keep the money in her purse but that's a small price to pay to recover all her other valuables.

💬 Tom

I lost my purse in a cab following a Christmas do a couple of years ago. I thought I would never see it or the big wad of notes I had taken out for Christmas shopping again, but three days later I had a call from the Hackney Carriage Lost Property Office in King's Cross. Honest cabbies can hand stuff in and for a small fee (e.g. a fiver) you say thanks and they give you your lost stuff back – hurray!

💬 Clairey

Please help me to find love. The summer is almost over and I'm still all alone. I've missed out on all the wonderful things you can do when you are a couple and it's summertime – holding hands and wandering through parks, strolling along the Thames etc. So with autumn around the corner, I would like to find someone to kick leaves and go to the Fireworks with.

🗨 Smurfette

Smurfette – sorry to say but you're presumably still single because you you're under the illusion that a smurfette looking for a smurf is cute and attractive? It is if you're nine.

I've been single for a few months too and was looking forward to meeting all these bright independent sexy Bridget Jones single types one reads about. Imagine my disappointment to find it tricky to have a sensible grown up conversation with any of you. Some of you even talk to your cats.

🗨 Mike

There's a central lost property office next to Baker Street tube station, which claims to handle stuff found on tubes, buses and cabs. Wicked idea, shame it hasn't been publicised.

🗨 Superflake

'FOUND'

I keep finding umbrellas – everywhere – on tubes, on buses, at bus stops, in gutters. I find big ones, small ones, ones that fire at 700 miles an hour when you press the button. In fact I'm vaguely worried that it's a curse. I feel like I'm being followed. I know that's impossible to be followed by an inanimate object, but that's how it feels. Or perhaps I'm the one doing the following, and I don't even know it. Oh God. Have I turned into a mentalist?

Katherine

To Katherine the Umbrella Finder: What we have here is deep-seated kleptomaniac tendencies. I'm sure you're aware of the Lighter Thieves. The people that go home after a night out with half a dozen lighters in their pockets that will later be added to the drawer in their bedroom that already contains 157. These people will protest their innocence when confronted with their crimes. They claim it's a reflex action. They didn't mean to do it, it just sort of happened. Something they can't help doing. Which is of small comfort to the decent honest folk who return them. Lighter Thieves are common. I have at least three as good friends.

But what we have here is an altogether new phenomenon. The Umbrella Thief. Umbrellas (like lighters) are the kind of things that just disappear. And before today I always wondered where. Now I know. It's people like Katherine stealing them! I think it must be some kind of magpie syndrome. Lighter Thieves are blinded by the fire. At a subconscious level they feel they must accrue as much of it as possible. Quite why you would be so attracted to umbrellas I'm not quite sure.

Is it the variety of colour? The new and exciting ways that they open? The variety of shapes and sizes? Perhaps an umbrella committed some horrible and unspeakable crime against you as a child? Or maybe you were born of an umbrella? Whatever it may be there is something deep down inside you forcing you to steal umbrellas. For the sake of humanity you must desist!

I lost five this winter alone! Leave be my umbrella!

🗨 **Sudonim**

Spotted

PUMPS

Those pesky empty petrol stations dotted around. They're like zits on our (my!) city. Why are they all being allowed to rot? Why is no-one knocking them down and building on them? If it was my petrol station I'd clear it out and build a skate park for the kids, or a communal garden for all the mums.

🗨 **Flash Bobby**

As an engineer, I feel it is my duty to explain a bit about derelict petrol stations. Yes, there is something very sinister and post-apocalyptic about these structures and yes, it is difficult to imagine how land so valuable as that in London can simply be left to waste.

Well, to explain, derelict petrol stations are the sort of things that make actuaries sweat under the collar and insurers rub their hands together. The vast tanks buried under ground, full of petrol vapour and set in reinforced concrete, are rather difficult and expensive to remove, while playing children can fall into them and smoking builders' mates can cause the sort of damage terrorist organisations crave for. So, they are fenced off, bricked up, locked down and simply left there.

💬 Friendly Geek

BELLS

Wondering if anybody can help? I keep seeing bells (about waist-high) on street corners around King's Cross.
They're made of cast iron and at first I thought they were to stop drivers cutting corners, but now I have seen some with bollards behind them. Are the bells unique to King's Cross, and what are they for? If anybody is interested you get to see quite a lot of them on the 91 bus route. The ones I have seen are on the junctions of Wharfedale Road/Caledonia Road, Euston Road/Ossulton Street (near the British Library), Euston Road/Churchway.

💬 Mandy

The bells I believe, are bollards, shortened to avoid restricting a driver's view of traffic around the corner.

I have seen them in other places in London. I have a feeling that the fact that they are next to normal bollards is due to the terrible habit of updating street furniture without removing the old lot, leaving things looking worse than when there was just one lot of old tatty furniture.

💬 Zed

The bells you see on the footway around King's Cross are known as 'Bell Bollards' and are designed to prevent vehicles mounting verges or footways. You will also notice half and quarter bell bollards scattered around. Some local authorities slap them all over the place. Tower Hamlets has a particular fetish for putting random bollards everywhere possible.

A minor point of note is the bell bollards are not sanctioned or permitted under highway regulations but their popularity has made the holder of the design patent a millionaire.

💬 Conehead

QUEUE

Every morning while on the number 26 bus from Waterloo to Spital Square, I pass a large, orderly queue forming outside India House on the Aldwych. Who are they, and why do they queue up there every morning?

💬 Lisa

These poor souls are queuing for a visa to visit India. I have endured the process three times myself. The whole thing takes the best part of a day and is the most amazingly antiquated process known to man, involving no end of forms, waiting, rubber stamps, tickets, chaos and almost no sign of a computer.

💬 Steve

I was just wondering if anyone has ever seen me on the tube and thought I was lovely?

💬 Helen

HOUSE OF REPUTE

Whilst wandering through the back streets of Soho in the pissing rain one Sunday, somewhere between Wardour Street and Charing Cross Road, I noticed signs in a couple of windows saying 'there are no prostitutes here' and something along the lines of 'if you have given money to anyone for this purpose we suggest you call the police'.

I can't remember the exact wording but it sounded like a bit of a scam going on with dodgy geezers taking cash in the street for 'personal' services and then sending people to a rogue address. Whatever next!

Little Lady B

It's a form of clipping, one of the oldest forms of sexual scamming known to mankind. Mug punter meets prostitute, hands over money and heads to the location said prostitute has told him he'll receive enlightenment at. Prostitute disappears, marvelling at mug punter's naivety. See Jake Arnott's excellent *He Kills Coppers* for more.

Linda Palermo

SURVIVE

I used to commute in to Paddington and admired every day the graffiti attributed to Banksy on the north side of the track just before Royal Oak station. It had his trademark monkey-faced royal uttering the inspired phrase 'Only the ridiculous survive'. It really agreed with me. Railtrack have long since painted it over, but I've started hankering for it again and despite a few mentions of it on the net I can't find a picture of it anywhere. I'd really like to have one. I meant to do it at the time, but you know... Can anyone help me get reacquainted?

☐ Iain

Banksy sells some prints and things via www.picturesonwalls.com. My personal fave is the 'Golf Sale'.

☐ cdouble

Iain, I guess you've had a look around his site at www.banksy.co.uk but it's possible that it may be archived there somewhere. He's also published a couple of collections of photos of his work called *Existencillism*, (at least the second one was). I would look through it to see if it's in there but some thieving bastard has nicked it, I'm afraid.

☐ Tiddles

It's good to talk...

FALLING DOWN

I was trotting down the escalator at Shepherd's Bush the other day, and overtook a curious looking gentleman with slicked hair and a sort of sideways tilt to his head. As I passed, he said: 'it's my birthday'. He said it quite loudly. There was no-one else on the escalator: he was speaking to me. But I kept my eyes fixed firmly forwards, and clattered on down towards the platform like the devil was at my heels. And it's been bugging me ever since. I didn't wish him 'happy birthday'. I didn't say it because I thought he might be a lunatic and slash at my throat with a sharpened spoon handle, like they learn in jail. I got scared. Because this is London, right? And in London we don't talk to anyone. Eyes down. Shut up. Keep moving. Keep moving. Don't speak. Don't wish a lonely gentleman 'happy birthday'. Don't smile at him. It's really sad. Then again, he probably had his fist clenched round a bread knife. Fucking nutter. Get out of my way!

Dixon

I know exactly what you mean. I can't abide the fact that we cannot talk to people around us in London purely because we don't know them. I really do feel trapped by this sometimes – no-one wants to talk to a stranger who approaches them in case the stranger is mad, and because of the fact that no-one talks, we think that anyone who does *must* be mad, because it's only mad people who talk to strangers in London, because no-one else ever does etc, etc.

I know people from other countries who've tried to have a

chat with strangers on the tube and have been greeted with horror. And I'm guilty myself – any time I've been approached by someone, I've always tried to react as normally as I can and be civil, while desperately hoping that they'll stop.

But the problem is that because tube-talkers very rarely have someone respond to them, when they find someone who will, it encourages them and they latch on to you. Having said that, I don't think anyone should be point-blank ignored – if someone talks, or wants to stop any of us in the street for charity or a questionnaire, I always think that the least we can do is reply, communicate, even if it's a 'no thanks'.

I really think it's a damn shame when people feel that they have to ignore other people.

💬 **Declan**

> I was just walking up Gloucester Road – it was nice and sunny, a man was enjoying a roll-up on the steps of a hotel, and a lady was wheeling her happy toddler along in a pushchair. Then I remembered that London is about to be blown up by terrorists.
>
> What a dull thought. I bought myself a fruit drink and a salad. Might as well die healthy.
>
> 💬 **Joel**

Maybe we could create a secret 'talking' society and wear 'LBL' badges on our lapels? This way we would know it's OK to approach and chat to any other wearer. It would have the added value of confusing the hell out of other less talkatives around us as we on-and-offed various tubes without any apparent connection or pattern.

💬 **Tonytone**

GOING UP

Some facts:

1) I live in Hampstead.

2) Hampstead has the deepest underground station.

3) The surface and the trains are linked by lifts.

4) I travel into work by tube.

5) Whenever I get into a lift (and I mean every time) I fantasize about what sort of a community would be formed by the people in the lift if we were suddenly, for some vaguely apocalyptic reason, to become the last people on earth. Who would emerge as leader? How soon before the first sexual encounter? What skills could each of us bring to a survival situation? Would I strike out on my own, and live a solitary life in a crudely built treehouse? Would I attempt to mate with any of my fellow lift-survivors? And if so, who?

Needless to say, it's fact number five that I'm most concerned about. As soon as the lift closes, the assessment begins. (I actually feel more comfortable in a packed lift, because I think the increased numbers would make for a more rounded society.) I'd quite like to be able to stop it, but I can't. My question is this: can anyone suggest any other lift-based nervous habits with which I might be able to depose my society-forming fantasy?

☐ Ben Lowe

Not specifically lift-related but more tube in general: I find that a couple of months playing that damned *Resident Evil* game on the PlaySatan has left me unable to complete a tube journey on my own without idly working out

a) the quickest routes from A to B to avoid the clutches of zombie commuters
b) how to get into the power room undetected
c) where the shotgun shells are etc.

I think that if the people sat next to me on the tube could see inside my head, they might move to a different carriage.

This has been going for about two years and I thought I was getting better but then I played that *Splinter Cell* thingy.

Now, I stride through the tunnels of Elephant and Castle
a) working out the best angles to shoot out security cameras; and
b) the best places to do split jumps and knock out unwitting tube employees etc. I don't seem to be able to stop. Does anyone have similar experiences? Is it just the crushing boredom of walking the same long underground rat-runs day in, day out and a mind looking desperately for escape via the medium of fantasy? Or am I just a sad twat?

◻ **Tiddles**

A little bit of both, I fear.

◻ **Mickey D**

TOOTH IS CHEAP

I've been reading about 'Bluejacking'– that is sending a message via Bluetooth to other mobile phones. Bluetooth is a short range radio networking type thingy that doesn't require you to be in range of your mobile network – which means it can work on the underground.

Although I've heard in the news about people doing this – has anyone actually tried it or been the recipient of a cryptic message on their phone? The range is about ten metres so you could potentially bounce messages between carriages on the tube.

 Sparky

I use this quite a lot on the tube, it livens up the journey. At the moment my phone is sending the message 'your flies are open.' The only thing is to try and keep a straight face.

 Stu

I've jollied up a few dull moments on the tube or waiting for people on Oxford Street by Bluejacking indiscriminate victims with messages such as 'got your number...'.

Beware though, when you are cooped up in your underground carriage: Remember that you don't know who will receive the message and that it will probably be the most tech'ed up person, not necessarily the good-looking bird/bloke sitting opposite that you've been eyeing up for the last five minutes.

Beware also that mobile phones have been hacked over Bluetooth, so leaving your Bluetooth enabled all the time might attract more attention than you expect.

 Wireless Hooligan

I tried out the Bluetooth thing this morning on the train to work, the underground and while getting a coffee in Victoria. I tried sending a picture to 'Bluetooth devices' but none of the phones that I found were connecting. Until I got to *Costa Coffee* in Victoria. My phone found a Nokia this, a Sony that and a Clare (original!), so I sent a picture of the platform at Westminster. How original.

💬 Julio

A brilliant place for this is *Selfridges* basement. Many enabled phones and space enough to hide and observe your victim. For more info check out www.bluejackq.com.

💬 **Pinksquid**

I would like to sincerely apologise to Mssrs Fakir, Kevin, Mags and T610, all of whom received highly odd Bluetooth messages from myself on Saturday night, during a trip to the *Hammersmith Apollo*. The confused expressions on Kevin's face at the District line particularly caused so much mirth that my asthma rekindled itself.

💬 **Simon Stacpoole**

To whoever stole my car stereo in Clapham the other night, I hope you enjoy it as much as I did. Oh, and that typewriter you nicked from the boot – I've been trying to find it a good home for ages.

💬 **South Of The River Girl**

Animal magic

FAT CAT

Does anyone else remember Tiddles, the hugely fat tabby cat that lived in the ladies toilet at Paddington station? My grandmother used to take me to see him; I remember being told that he arrived as a kitten, and then spent all his time being fed and thoroughly spoilt by the attendants, growing bigger and bigger, until he rarely walked (he did look too enormous to get far) and became a bit of a celebrity (in Paddington station anyway). I was small, so I expect he seemed more impressively large. I can't be making this up, can I? No-one else ever seems to know what I am talking about...

Pockettiger

No, you are not making up the enormously fat cat in the Ladies loos at Paddington station.

My Dad would take me to visit Tiddles every time we went to Cornwall way back in 1979–81. According to my sister, the toilet attendant was a little on the heavy side too. As I type, I have a photo of Tiddles that my Dad purchased for me from the attendant which says on the back 'My name is Tiddles (I am a boy). I live in the Ladies loo at Paddington station. My weight is 28lbs. I will be 11 years old in October 1981. I eat rabbit, kidneys, cod steak, lambs tongue and chicken. I can walk, run and jump when I feel like it!'

Gooneretle1

Yep, Tiddles was real. But he's not now. He died (of obesity) in 1983.

 Tiddler

I was standing with a couple of colleagues outside our office having a ciggy when there's this seagull call.

Next thing it strafes – and I do mean strafes – the pavement about three feet behind my mate and continues to circle. Needless to say, we dived for cover. You would not believe the amount of white goo one bird can produce. Two days passed and another colleague, previously unaware of our new lurking menace, pulls up in her car and parks outside. Within minutes of parking outside the office, the same (we assume) seagull has coated her car from bonnet to boot in shit with military precision.

It completely missed the vehicles either side of hers and not a drop of guano fell anywhere other than on her car. This is getting beyond a joke. Make no mistake, these are focused attacks. We're all buying air guns.

G

GONE FISHING

I was walking across Wandsworth Bridge the other day, when my eye was caught by a large black-ish blob on the river bank. I stood there trying to work out whether it was a big tarpaulin filled with jelly or something, when it suddenly waddled up the riverbank to a warmer spot. It was a seal! In the Thames! is this a normal occurrence?

Willis

I have seen the seal too. My step-dad works down on the barges on the Thames, near the *Rutland* in Hammersmith. He/she is lovely, and apparently keeps popping up down that way. I'm not sure how many seals one usually spots lurking about in the Thames, but by the size of it, it looks like she/he is the only one eating all the... are there even any fish in the Thames?

Lou Ling

Seals are indeed back in the Thames. I noticed a couple over the summer – sightings which inevitably prompted arguments about whether it could really be a seal – was it perhaps not an otter? Or a beaver? But they are definitely seals. Ask a diver: www.divernet.com/news/items/seal030200.htm.

thefaris

I was just as shocked when I saw a large seal contentedly sunning itself on a Thames islet in Chiswick, Willis. I'm willing to bet that was the same seal as the one you spotted in Wandsworth. Anyone else see this seal along the Thames? I can only assume it travelled all the way through London.

Rombo

There are a disproportionate number of men with limps working in the City. I point this out to other City workers and they agree but nobody can explain it.

Con

Twenty years ago, water quality in Old Father Thames was horrible. Nowadays, however, the Thames is regarded as one of the cleanest metropolitan estuaries in the world – so much so that even creatures like trout are returning to London's waterways. Some of you might even remember seeing a dolphin playing around under Blackfriars Bridge last year?

Fishy Lips

Yes, there are fish in the Thames! Incredible to believe but it's true. There's even salmon returning, but after a good period about ten years ago the numbers have dropped off recently – possibly due to the seals? My lecturers even told me the Thames was one of the cleanest rivers in Britain, though common sense and the crap left at low tide tells me that was probably rubbish. But have you noticed it doesn't smell too bad?

One thing though, Rombo: 'I can only assume it travelled all the way through London.' How else could it have got there? Hitched a lift from Southend? I want to know.

BiologyMan

HORSE

I live on Great Western Road in W9. About once a month a group of soldiers on horses pull a cannon down the road while I'm having breakfast. The first time this happened was on Guy Fawkes' night last year, and I assumed it was something to do with a fireworks display, but since then they have come past about once a month – sometimes more often. Does anyone know where they come from or where they are going?

Suzy

The horses and field guns trooping past Suzy's house in W9 are from the Household Cavalry. They exercise every day on a patch of ground at the Scrubs Lane side of Wormwood Scrubs. To get there from their barracks, they traipse through the streets of W11/W10/W9, taking various routes – they've done this for decades, now. I've seen them as far north as Kilburn Park Road/Carlton Drive (NW6) and in the mid-70s they used to thunder down St Quintin's Avenue in W10 about twice a week, at breakfast time.

To my eternal shame, my mum and other earnest seventies hippies of the time would rush out following their departure and collect up all the fresh, steaming fertilizer, for the garden.

Meg

UNCONFIRMED SIGHTINGS

As I was wandering through Green Park a week or two ago, I saw a man being followed by a crow. He was walking across the grass and every few yards the crow would flap after him. The man would then wave his arms manically and keep walking. The crow would stop, wait, then follow him again. Strange. Was this his pet crow? Was it just a highly intelligent wild crow that has learnt how to annoy people? Or perhaps a sniffer crow, trained by the Royal Parks Constabulary?

💬 Flatpack

Not sure about Crow Man but has anyone seen Batdog? He stalks the streets of Maida Vale. They say owners grow to look like their pets and I think I've found Batman's canine companion. A white bulldog shaped dog with black markings on his head. The black markings look JUST like a Batman mask, he even has the same pointy ears.

He's always running and panting heavily, where is he going? Has anyone else seen him? There's also a little old Jack Russell in our park that wears a muzzle that makes him look like Hannibal the cannibal.

💬 Spaniel

And finally

THE HEIST

I watched a video of *The Score* on Saturday. It was quite a dull movie, in which Robert de Niro, a long-time jewel thief, decided to take on one last job so he could retire from his life of crime and settle down with an air hostess. And it made me want to have a life of crime from which I could one day retire. I want to plan a heist. Ideally one in which no-one gets bonked on the head, or shot in the thigh. I don't mind crawling through tunnels or along ventilation shafts – provided we've gone over the blueprints meticulously in advance. In fact, going over blueprints is an absolute must. I also want to hire a lock-up, with an old Ford Granada in it, and to have meetings there where one of us gets cold feet about the whole operation, but is talked back on board. Who will join me? And what's our first target?

Raffles

In response to Raffles, I would be bang up for robbing a bank or similar institution. I recently applied for voluntary redundancy and got turned down, so I need to do something a little more drastic in order to leave the company with a sizeable pay-off.

I assume we can safely rely on all LBL readers to act as potential alibis? Also, we may need to borrow a fast car from someone. Any other ideas?

Billy the Kid

I should like to join Raffles on the heist. Or, The Heist as we must now refer to it. It has long been an ambition of mine to meticulously plan and execute the perfect crime. I assume that this will be the perfect heist?

I'd also like permission to cover my face in that special mud/make up soldiers and master criminals use when we do the crawling through tunnels bit. And of course, at some point someone must be locked into the boot of the old Ford Granada. Will have a think about targets.

 Magpie

What happens to old hairdressers? I've never been past a salon and seen any worker aged over about 40. Who's a hairdresser? Come on; share the secrets of your trade. Do you kill them off?

🖵 Lem

Count me in. Where do I sign? There must be a counter-plot for one of us to rip the other one off. I suggest that one of us has a connection with a man in a government department called 'Bounton' who goes about dressed in a pin stripe suit and bowler hat, reminiscent of the dodgy Secret Service characters in *The Icpress File*.

Said contact will link us to a cigar racket that involves Cuba, the world's smallest diamond tiepin and Lloyds' Shipping. One of us needs all the wedge from the heist (as it'll be a bank job or nicking the takings from a fancy London jewellers or some such) to finance a further rip-off which will make everyone fit for a spell in Easy Street, Acapulco. Mine's a large Margarita with umbrella.

🖵 Gail

Raffles, count me. I have considered a variety of potential roles and would like to put myself down as the triple-crossing whizzkid who gets to act like a mong throughout the length of the heist. I will accept nothing less than 100% of the spoils, but am prepared to be outwitted and receive 0%, consoling myself with an anguished 'Gah!' before legging it.

💬 Andy H

HOOKY?

Does anyone work on a market stall? Is it like they make it look on _EastEnders_, or do find yourself rolling your eyes and tutting at the screen?
And how much, if any, of your gear is 'hooky'?

💬 Luke

My dad used to work on a market stall, selling fruit. None of it, to the best of my knowledge, was hooky.

💬 Katherine

EYES DOWN

I want to start a club, and this is the club that I want to start: The London Wild Grass Appreciation Society. I've always had a sort of background interest in grasses, but never pursued it. Except that once, while still at school, I bought a secondhand Collins book of grasses – or something like that – but I didn't do anything with it, which is a shame, because if I had then I could be a botanist right now, instead of a Civil Servant.

My idea for the LWGAS is that we'd meet up, with pads and magnifying glasses (for identification purposes) and wander around a park for a bit at weekends and spot grasses, like Vetch and Cocksfoot and Timothy Grass. And then we'd sit and drink some wine or beer and compare notes. And perhaps people would make presentations, on subjects like 'How To Identify Fescues' or 'My Favourite Bit of Streatham Common' – which would be greeted with rounds of applause. I don't really know what would happen. I don't want to be President or anything – I just want to be a member. Or perhaps Treasurer. Any thoughts anyone?

Joseph T

Get in touch with Islington Ecology Centre, Gillespie Park (local nature reserve), 191 Drayton Park, London N15 1PH. Telephone: 020 7354 5162 Fax: 020 7288 1717. They occasionally have walks and talks about grasses – apparently, there are a couple of rare species (varieties?) on site.

Frederick

KITE

On a recent bank holiday Sunday, after a so-so house party at my shared flat, we decided to fly a kite. It was 4am and there was no wind, but it seemed like a good idea at the time. In the end we just watched the sun come up, which was lovely.

Unfortunately, on the way back, my housemate screwed up the fence climbing and fell. He snapped his forearm just below the elbow and gushed blood all over the place. You'll be glad to know that he is much better now, and has lots of steel in his arm. However, two weeks later, the blood is still on the pavement. At the time, the ambulance driver said someone would come and clean it up, but after all the sun we've had recently, it's very well baked on.

So, keep your eyes peeled if you're on a 133 or 333 bus as you go past Oval church and tube station. On the pavement next to Kennington Park is a stark reminder not to fly kites at 4am.

💬 Anon

Anon's revelation that he was a kite flyer last week reminded me how much I hate kite flyers. Park-wrecking bastards, forever threatening your picnic and spilling your beers with huge divebombing falcons and shit.

But then again, I probably hate them because I play soft-ball in parks and probably fuck up people's lives even more than the kite guy does. So, come on LBLers, who pisses you off more, kite flyers or softball players?

💬 Linda

I can assure Linda that softball players are by far the most irritating species of parklife. I play football in Regent's Park once a week. Last summer the part of the park we normally play in was colonised by two groups of softball players. One of these groups included a couple of intensely anal Americans – I'm sure they would have contended they were playing base*barl,* but, like, whatever.

Anyway, there we were playing our normal game of football with a couple of our bikes parked behind the goals when one of them came over and asked us to move our bikes because they were in their playing area. Well, he was right – our bikes were *on the boundary*. So visualise, if you please, a softball pitch marked out in a *public* park.

I'm not going to go into vulgar acreage, but it's quite big. Now think of the area that half a bicycle wheel takes up on the boundary of that pitch. Oooooooh, they made us mad. And we took great pleasure in telling them to shut up, and booting the ball past the goal onto their pitch for the rest of the evening. How brave we felt, 16 young strapping lads passive-aggressively encroaching on their playing area.

Heady days.

💬 **Camelpoo**

Food and Drink

London may not be *quite* ready to take its place amongst the great European culinary capitals, but we're getting there. And when it comes to alcohol consumption and hangover-busting fry-ups, we're already the undisputed world leaders. In this section, LBLers offer their expert advice 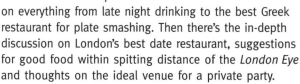 on everything from late night drinking to the best Greek restaurant for plate smashing. Then there's the in-depth discussion on London's best date restaurant, suggestions for good food within spitting distance of the *London Eye* and thoughts on the ideal venue for a private party.

And what food and drink section would be complete without mentioning the capital's finest late night karaoke bars? Not this one, that's for damn sure.

The morning after, the night before

BEFORE

I would like information on places in central-ish London where you can drink after hours without paying exorbitant prices, or being forced to share a dodgy illegal drinking den in darkest Soho with 300 other people, constantly awaiting the arrival of the police.

I can recommend *Quinns* in Camden (on Kentish Town Road) which is open till 2am on Thurs/Fri/Sat. A list of these would be gold-dust I reckon.

💬 **Mills**

Oxygen in Leicester Square is generally open until 1–2am. Pricey, but not exorbitant, and generally not too busy considering its location.

💬 John-James

The *Phoenix Artist's Club*, Charing Cross Road, underneath the *Phoenix Theatre* (where Blood Brothers has been on for twenty-eight-million years). If you get there before 10pm, then Thursday through Saturdays you can drink there until 3am. West End pub prices (although you can only get bottled beer after about eleven). There is a membership scheme, for about £25 a year, through which you can guarantee late entrance. It's a cool place.

💬 Linda

London is full of hideous, bland, anodyne bars. Many of them used to be fine pubs, only to have been hi-jacked by soulless marketing robots with an *Ikea* catalogue and a collection of Hed Kandi albums. Soon, anywhere with any character will have been eradicated by those motivated only by profit, whilst those who hate the *All Bar One*s of this world have to stay at home and drink or tolerate establishments full of self-important wankers. It is for this reason that I didn't mention the *Phoenix Artist's Club* when the appeal went around for after hours drinking clubs. If, in time, the *Phoenix* becomes a *Wetherspoons*-alike, at least I know who to blame.

 Jeff's Vodka & Soda

If Jeff knows who to blame if the *Phoenix* turns into a *Wetherspoons*-alike then I'll know who to blame when it turns into an elitist establishment full of exclusive wankers who don't want their secret being known by others. Share the knowledge Jeff.

Linda

I've been wondering about the validity of the *Queen Vic* in *EastEnders*. Why has there never (to my knowledge) been an Antipodean working behind the bar?

GG

The Spanish Bar on Hanway Street, between Tottenham Court Road and Oxford Street – open until 1am on Sundays. *The Blue Lion* on Gray's Inn Road – open until 2am every week day. Neither of them super-salubrious, but *The Blue Lion* does have a pool table. And serves food too.

Drinker

All-night pubs in London are cropping up all over the place.
O'Neills near Covent Garden, for example: get in there before
11pm (about 10pm is perfect) because then they lock the
door. No-one can come in, only outbound traffic. Although
if you have a mate with a mobile joining your group late
on you can normally open the door when the bar staff
aren't looking.

Basically, they're open until the last person leaves,
although they have to close before 6am. Turn up with a large
bunch of mates there on a Tuesday night and go back home
next morning on the tube!

☐ **Tris2000**

It's always hard finding local after-hours drinking spots.
In Battersea I usually end up at *Castilla* on Battersea Rise
– it's a good bar but it does tend to have an atmosphere
reminiscent of the Northern line during rush hour. Does anyone
know of anywhere in the Battersea/Clapham/Wandsworth
vicinity where you can get a drink after 11 in a bar that
wouldn't make a sardine feel claustrophobic?

☐ **Gentleman Loner**

The Twelve Pins in Finsbury Park stays open until at least
2am, has no entry fee and no bar staff. It's also stuffed full
of extremely pissed and ramshackle Irish drinkers, who
nonetheless are extremely friendly and welcoming. Plus, with
it being Finsbury Park, there are lots of places to go for a
post-pub falafel.

☐ **Jimmy H**

My vote goes to *Matt and Matt* on Upper Street. It's an oasis
amongst the selection of chain bars and oh-so-stylish

over-priced fascist-bouncer rip-off joints in the area. It's open until 2am on Fridays and Saturdays (£4 to enter after 10pm) and 1am on school nights (free all night), and has a good selection of reasonably priced drinks, including yummy flavoured vodkas (a bit 90s, I know, but you still can't go wrong with Bounty vodka). It's classy without being pretentious, and tends to get a fairly chilled, laid-back crowd. Plus great live music and open DJ nights, and the friendliest bar staff in North London.

🖵 **Kaffkins**

I'm loathe to give out such information, but share the wealth and all that... *The Jazz Bar* in Dalston is a winner; small, lively and seemingly open all hours, selling decent booze and playing jazz and easy listening, it's down one of the side roads next to Dalston Kingsland station.

Obviously most people would be unlikely to want to start investigating side streets in Dalston late at night, but for those brave enough, sweet, sweet booze and a late night laugh will be your reward.

🖵 **Dirtos**

My late night London bar is *Sevilla Mia*, a basement bar on Hanway Street, between Oxford Street and Tottenham Court Road. Gets very crowded – it's very small – but get there before 11pm and you'll get a seat, and it stays open well into the night.

🖵 **chaz b**

As someone has already nominated *Sevilla Mia* on Hanway Street, I've got to go for *Castilla* on Battersea Rise, just down from Clapham Junction. Officially open for drinking and superb tapas Monday–Thursday until midnight, and Friday–Saturday until 2am, but more often than not, until the last person leaves. The *Castilla* atmosphere somehow manages to combine a friendly welcome with the impression that you've stumbled into a Spanish *Goodfellas* and you're a made guy. They don't open on Sundays but after a late Saturday there you'll understand why.

💬 **auawsha**

The best late night bar has to be *The Strong Rooms* off Curtain Road in Shoreditch. Not dominated by Hoxton flicks, it is just somewhere for people to go to have a nice drink away from the crowds after other places have closed. They often have live bands in the basement going on late and if it's too noisy inside you can stand in the quiet cobbled courtyard outside. It is cheap and unpretentious and when it's quiet you kind of feel like you're in an old fashioned canteen. Stays open till the last person leaves.

   Great!

💬 **nb**

I nominate the *Tongue and Groove* bar in Brixton as the finest late-night watering hole (south of the river at least). It's open until 4am at weekends and the door charge is nominal. The bar staff are friendly and mix a mean and not too pricey mojito. It's one of the few Brixton bars which is neither white or black and there's a refreshing lack of attitude inside. It's got a massive leather lounge area, which is nice. And there's a great party vibe on Fridays and Saturdays. Do I have shares? No. Should I have a direct debit? Yes.

💬 **Blakey**

AFTER

**Not that I'm a heavy drinker, you understand.
But when I woke up this afternoon, I found myself
wondering where London's best hangover breakfast
might be found. Or London's best breakfast generally.
Any suggestions?**

⌨ Paul

Best breakfast in London is found in the Spanish café at
the top end of Queensway. They do an English, which is
excellent, or a Spanish fry-up, which is essentially the same
but with a kind of chorizo sausage. They also do the best
hot chocolate in London. Melt chocolate, add cream, stir,
stand spoon straight up and serve.

⌨ dwp

It's got to be *The Boiled Egg & Soldiers* on Northcote Road,
just down from Clapham Junction. They serve huge meat
or vegetarian all-day breakfasts along with a sometimes
much-needed Sunday morning Bloody Mary. There's even
outside seating on the pavement so you can watch the
goings-on in the street market as you pig out.

⌨ auawsha

The Mess Café in Hackney (on the road that leads from
Hackney Downs to Hackney Central station) has easily the
tastiest cooked breakfast I've had in a long time. Really good
quality sausages and bacon, and they'll do your eggs the
way you like them. They do some yummy milkshakes and
smoothies too.

⌨ House Mouse

My nomination has to be *Goodfellas Deli*, 50 Lamb Conduit Street. From the outside it looks like a basic deli counter but it has a wee courtyard out back where you can have a full cooked brekky with big chunky sausages and all the rest, with a choice of brown granary bread instead of fluffy white if you are so inclined.

🗨 **Trev**

I nominate *Mario's Café* in Kentish town. Other than the fact it has been mentioned in a Saint Etienne song, they do the best breakfast in North London at a semi-reasonable price (I think it was £7 last time I went). They use the best organic and top quality products for the eggs, bacon and sausages, etc, but they do a really good Eggs Benedict, far better than I've had in some posher restaurants up-town. And the staff are very friendly.

🗨 **Sachin**

The *Drayton Park Café* in N5 is great – always full of local workmen, and they know a thing or two about a decent fry-up. Huge plates of quality food for about £4.50, and decent veggie options (including bubble 'n' squeak!) if you're not inclined towards meat. Top hash browns too.

🗨 **Katkins**

Keston Lodge in Upper Street for a lazy Sunday morning treat (£5–8 depending on what you have) or *Sim Sim's* on Blackstock Road for weekdays.

🗨 **RC**

I'm planning to take the wife to London for our first anniversary and need some ideas for must-see stuff to do and non-extortionate places to stay. I'm thinking nice spots on the river for a moonlit wander where I'm not going to get stabbed by a crack whore, little out of the way places that don't normally show up on the tourist radar and things that aren't full of pseudo-middle-class ponces that cost the earth. Yes I've looked on Google, no I haven't seen anything that inspires me. Any suggestions of entertaining shows that don't require a degree in satirical literature would be greatly appreciated.

💬 I'd Visit But I'd Never Live There

Any chance of telling 'I'd Visit But I'd Never Live There' not to bother visiting London? His sad attempt to be cool and knowing (stabbed by crack whores indeed) make me think that the brilliance of London is wasted on him. For a safe experience with the wife I suggest he never leaves home.

💬 mickyw

Entirely impractical unless you live in E17/E10, or are escaping from Whipps Cross hospital, but the 24-hour burger van between Walthamstow and Leytonstone is my best brekkie nomination. Lovely burgers/English breakfast baps, that you blend together in any combination for a delicious brekkie, that you can eat next to Epping Forest's boating pond, whilst feeding the geese and swans. The food is great; big fat proper ingredients, and on a sunny day it's gorgeously scenic, and quiet enough to forget you're in London. It's just a shame that it's bloody ages from anywhere, except for a few lucky locals and the occasional passing lorry drivers. I recommend the quarter-pounder with egg, cheese, bacon, sausage and mushrooms. And a tissue to clean up the mess.

💬 Gizzard

In an otherwise dismal area for interesting food, *The Tollgate Café* in the square across from Archway station offers an excellent breakfast – full English in large and small sizes, veggie pancakes with fried banana and a few eggy things (I don't like eggs much, so I'm short on details). They've always got the day's newspapers lying around and there's a nice patio out back. They've got a nice selection of fresh goodies for those with a sweet tooth as well.

💬 Chz

The Odd Spot in Hammersmith, over the road from the Riverside Studios, a proper greasy spoon, with proper food. Wonderful sausages, excellent tea and a full English that will see you right for at least 48 hours. Quite often full of rowers from the dodgy Hammersmith clubs. I'm only jealous as I row in Putney and we don't have such a good place to go for our brekkie.

💬 loaf

The Londesborough, Barbauld Road, N16 (Stoke Newington) does a superb, but not cheap (£7), breakfast of a weekend. Chargrilled sausages, bacon, two eggs, 'ranch style' potatoes (small cubes fried), two bits of chunky toast and tomatoes. Very nice indeed I can assure you.

💬 Dirtos

The Euro Café on Drummond Street. We've been going there with our sports club for years. The food is brilliant after a hard morning's training on a Saturday, and we even get free cups of tea!

💬 juicy

The Greek breakfast in the café on Muswell Road (near the Broadway, near corner) in Muswell Hill is exceptional and will probably do you for the rest of the day. Good atmosphere, good food and great staff in this bright, high ceiling'd caff.

💬 Damian

Banners in Crouch End do huge delicious breakfasts; the usual fry-up, veggie options, kedgeree, kippers... Perfect with a jug of frozen margarita. Always pretty busy though.

💬 pockettiger

Another good bet is *Café San Siro* at the foot of Highgate West Hill. Italian-run, but English content, and it's where the cabbies go, so can you ask for more? Yummy.

💬 pussinboots

Fox Reformed on Stoke Newington Church Street is a fabulous pub – bit pricey but worth it for the nice, calm atmosphere and heated beer garden. Does great French food too.

💬 Little G

The *Blue Brick Café* on Fellbrigg Road in East Dulwich is the best damn greasy spoon I've come across. Their full English comes with a big old slab of Bubble and Squeak or if you have chips they are the sort that come from real potatoes that have never seen the inside of a chest freezer. And toast from proper unsliced bread. Thankfully it's not too near my gaff or I'd be like Rik Waller by now.

🗨 **Breakfastfiend**

Undoubtedly the best place to go for breakfast in London is *Maggie's Café* in Lewisham. You choose as much as you like from the varied breakfast menu whilst listening to Elvis or a Motown compilation and lovely ladies come round and constantly fill up your tea or coffee cup all for £4. Brilliant! The service is fast and friendly, Maggie herself with her Irish charm and sparkle comes round to make sure you have everything you need and also to fill up your tea or coffee cup. It's a wonderful experience, like going to an old aunty or your nan's house and being spoilt rotten. I love it!

🗨 **Zoe**

It's got to be *Maggie's Café* in Lewisham. Ask for the special sauce.

🗨 **James W**

Best breakfast in London is undoubtedly to be found at *Basement Jo's* on Brixton Hill. Only a short bus ride or walk from Brixton tube, all the food is freshly cooked to order (so sometimes there is a bit of a wait), they have both an inside and outside area, the cafe is clean and full of interesting things on the wall, and they are very friendly and chatty. It is also one of the few places I know of that still does bubble 'n' squeak. Word on the street is that they also do an exceptional Sunday roast, though I have yet to try this. I never have breakfast anywhere else.

🗨 **William**

Eating out

LUNCH

I'm planning on taking my Mum on the *London Eye* and out for lunch for her birthday next weekend and am looking for some advice on where to take her. I'm looking for somewhere within walking distance from the *Eye* and not too expensive that cooks good food and has a welcoming atmosphere. Any suggestions?

🗨 **Kirstie**

For the kind lady taking her mum for lunch by the *London Eye*, you could try *Fish!* (on the other side of *County Hall*) for slightly pricey but superb fish dishes, or the lovely *Yo! Sushi* (next to *Fish!*) for the perfect conveyer belt dining experience (also pretty quiet at lunchtimes), or even the fab *People's Palace* in the *Royal Festival Hall*, kinda expensive but great food and a lovely view of the river.

🗨 **Costumekitten**

For a good place to go for lunch within walking distance of the *Eye* I can highly recommend *Gabriel's Wharf*. It's a five to ten minute walk along the South Bank (it's near the Oxo Tower) and is a cute little collection of restaurants that appear very out of place amongst the rest of the South Bank's scenery.

From what I can remember prices are pretty reasonable but unfortunately I haven't had the opportunity to go therefor a while. Added bonus is that if you carry on walking a bit further you can nip to the *Globe* and round the *Tate Modern* with your mum too!

🗨 **Nick Nocks**

I had lunch at *The People's Palace* restaurant in the *Royal Festival Hall* on my birthday after a flight on the *Eye* – it was a special deal with the *Eye*. Food's excellent, and there are lovely views over the Thames.

💬 Deborah

Tas Pide on New Globe Walk is a great Turkish place. It's about a 15-minute walk from the *London Eye* but the walk is along the banks of the Thames and you go past the *Tate Modern* and the *Globe Theatre* and it's a really nice stroll after being cooped up in the *Eye* for half an hour.

💬 Jo

SOY

I'd be glad to know, if someone could tell me, which Chinese restaurant to go to in Chinatown.

I must have eaten there a dozen times, and had some good meals, some bad meals and some excellent meals, but I don't have it firmly fixed in my mind where to go. Or where not to go. I'm bored of the fact that when I go there to eat, it's always with the same sense of unknowing. Are there one or two restaurants there that someone could recommend?

💬 Hungry Jim

Hungry Jim should not go to any of the Chinese restaurants in Chinatown – quality varies wildly not just between them but within each one from month to month.

Instead, he should go to one of the *Royal Chinas* or to *Phoenix Palace*, on Baker Street and just off Dorset Square respectively. Real Chinese food, not tourist rubbish.

💬 Stuart

In response to Hungry Jim's quest for Chinese food in Chinatown (started in the right place, at least), you all (yes, all, dammit) must visit the *Friendly Inn* at 47 Gerrard Street (behind the fire station on Shaftesbury Avenue). It is run by a complete lunatic of a woman who will greet you effusively and spout the most inane bollocks at you. Charming.

The best bit, however, is the 'special tea'. Just ask for it after 11pm and see what you get. Champion.

🗨 Growler

There is a cellar below the *Leather Exchange* pub in Bermondsey that stretches right along the road. It used to be a mortuary and the stone beds are still there.

Me and my mate tried to explore it once by Zippo light, but got too freaked out and had to retreat. Apparently they used to lynch people in the pub.

🗨 GG

Can anyone recommend a good central-ish cheese and wine bar/restaurant? I heard about one by the river once but despite my efforts I can't find any sign of it on the net.

🗨 Ali

Gordon's on Villiers Street is surely the best wine bar in London as long as you are not too tall or don't mind not being able to stand up. The wine is incredible and the atmosphere is terribly left bank. They do a great cheese platter as well.

🗨 Sophie

The bar Ali's talking about is probably the bar just up from
Embankment tube on Villiers Street. It's called *Gordon's* and
is the first building on the right, just after the park. You enter
through a small door and immediately descend into a sort
of French-style bar, covered in newspaper cuttings. As you
enter, the food (cheese, pickles etc) is just in front of you.
If you follow it round to the left you will get to the bar
which stocks a wide selection of wine and ports, many sold
by the glass. However if there is more than one of you,
I'd suggest that you buy a bottle as it's very difficult to
traverse from your table to the bar when the place gets
busy. The best seats (as long as you're not over 6'6") is in
the old railway tunnel. The ceiling is very low and everything
has been blackened by the candles (or maybe painted
black). This is a fantastic bar but come early if you want
a table.

🗨 **Eddie**

I'm almost tempted not to tell, because I love the place
so much, but you could try *Beaujolais* on Litchfield Street,
just off Charing Cross Road. It was the first French wine bar
in London 20-odd years ago, and is still run by a mate of
the original owner. They'll let you try wines before you order
and if you describe what you like, they'll find something
to match. They do great cheese and olives, too. Only problem?
It's the size of a matchbox, so get there early and expect to
be tightly squeezed in.

For somewhere less intimate and more modern-looking,
why not try *Hamptons* on Whitcomb Street (I think), behind
Leicester Square. Again a good selection of wine, and a good
cheese platter.

Final recommendations? *Gordon's* near Embankment, although that's always packed and the *Tappit Hen* on William IV Street, between Strand/Charing Cross Road.

🗨 robram

Café Des Amis in Covent Garden does fabulous cheese and wine. It has a restaurant but if I were you, I would simply go to the bar area where they have an excellent wine list and a platter of delicious (albeit a tad pricey) cheeses. The atmosphere is very cosy and chilled and the staff are lovely. It is a bit short on seats, so if it's a school night don't go too late. Also, don't be put off by the fact that it's in Covent Garden – it's on Hanover Place, tucked away down a side street so is never rammed with tourists and their retina-burningly bright leisurewear.

🗨 Aunt Flo

If you're a fan of Yum Cha, then the very best that I have found that London has to offer is *Joy King Lau* on Leicester Street, just off Leicester Square. Food is always on the money, great range, always a seat. This was my regular Sunday lunch for more months than I care to remember when I was living in Marylebone.

🗨 Tony

GREEK TO ME

Can anyone suggest a nice (and not too pricey) Greek restaurant in the centre of town? I need it for a dinner date. I suppose low lighting and intimate nooks would be on my wish-list as well. Plate-breaking I can take or leave. Actually, having said that, I'm probably not into the whole crockery-smashing thing. Not sure I understand it, really. Seems like a dreadful waste – although I bet they buy bulk. Seconds too, most likely.

💬 **Chris**

Nice Greek restaurant would be *The Real Greek* in Hoxton Market N1. It's a bit pricey but a good date place – well I wouldn't mind be taken there, and the food is more interesting than merely moussaka.

💬 **Mark**

My message is not helpful at all because I don't know any good restaurant in London (I live in another city) but I can assure you that this 'smashing' thing it does not happen in Greece any more. During 60s (I think) it was a kind of expression for someone who wanted to show that he/she was in a great mood and could even smash dishes (usually after drinking a lot). It was quite surprising for me (I am from Greece) to see that in UK people still doing it.

Don't believe them (this kind of restaurant) and enjoy the nice food (if it is nice because I had bad experience trying Greek food here). I hope you find a good restaurant.

💬 **Natasha**

Efes in Great Titchfield Street is like stepping back in time. In Camden on Bayham Street there are a whole selection. My fave is *Andy's*, which is very homely and does weekend plate-smashing.

🗩 **M1lls**

Costas, in Notting Hill (Hillgate Street, W8), is a great little Greek restaurant. The first time we went, we felt like we'd stepped into a scary 'locals-only' kind of place. The second time, we had magically become locals. The food is good, simple homey stuff and not too dear but I've no idea about authenticity or Greek vs Cypriot or anything. Sorry.

🗩 **Billy**

ICES

Can anyone tell me if there's anywhere in South London that sells mint choc chip ice cream? And I don't mean that Haagen Dazs/Ben & Jerry's type of stuff. Real proper mint choc chip, where the ice cream is the colour of green Tic Tacs and the choc chips should really be called chocolate flavoured chip facsimiles.

If mint choc chip's gone then it's only a matter of time until raspberry ripple and Neapolitan end up in the giant cone in the sky. Then we're left with a choice between vanilla or Belgian chocolate pecan toffee marshmallow rum surprise.

🗩 **Gromski**

Mint choc chip ice cream – I am pretty sure you can get some at *Marine Ices* in Chalk Farm. My mum used to go there as a little girl and it is still rocking today. Proper Gellati.

🗩 **Rachie**

I got some from *Iceland* in New Cross last year.

🗨 **Fishface**

Mint choc chip ice cream has never been away. My kids eat it all the time, most recently in Kensington Gardens from the stall by the playground that used to be usable but now has the Diana brand name and is unbelievably overcrowded. You can buy boxes of it almost anywhere.

🗨 **Billy**

The best thing about Germany in summer is the myriad of local ice cream cafés. Often run by Italian-German couples, these independent places sell a wide menu of carefully crafted, yet grossly proportioned sundaes at reasonable prices. In London, I only know of dingy franchised cafés selling Unilever subsidiary branded rubbish. The comparison couldn't be sadder. Is there a decent ice cream café in London?

🗨 **Alex**

Zilli Café on Brewer street does possibly the best ice cream I've ever tasted in London. I like to pop round there from work in the summer and walk slooooowly back, nothing like a good bit of ice cream as a good excuse to skive!

🗨 **Eggplant**

Marine Ices, at the bottom end of Haverstock Hill. opposite Chalk Farm tube station, has been serving genuine Italian ice creams for over seventy years. I've been going there for over forty and quite simply it's the best ice cream this side of Naples.

Food and coffee's not bad either. Walls are crammed out with plaques showing famous names who have eaten there in the past. Also popular for children's parties in the daytime.

Not cheap at £1.10 a scoop or £3–4 for the more exotic dishes but what do you expect for quality water ices using only fruit pulp or in season crop, as well as a range of the more fattening variety sundaes and knickerbocker glories? They do ice cream floats as well. About thirty to forty different flavours. And they do take-away in tubs, so best to arrive with a cool box or bag if your freezer has got room.

🗩 Pete

It's a date

WHERE TO GO?

I'd very much like to have some suggestions for a restaurant which will fit these criteria:

1) Suitable for taking a girl on her birthday. Not too flashy but intimate without being overbearing I would say.

2) I am a struggling journo so £80–100 absolute tops, preferably even less without looking cheap, including a healthy alcohol quotient (I never trust newspaper reviews where they seem to manage on one half bottle between 5 when totting up prices).

3) Cuisine is fairly open but maybe along the lines of seafood. Personally I like a good feed so none of that nouvelle malarkey.

Also, are all the lastminute.com type offers for cheap meals at *The Ivy* and so forth rubbish? Someone must have tried them – what's the catch? Seats by the lavatory and bread and water only or something?

🗩 Laurence

I recommend *Vasco* and *Piero's* on Poland Street. Not too expensive, great food, works a treat for dating.

💬 **Ed**

Oh God yes! I know where you could take her: *Andrew Edmunds* on Lexington Street W1 (020 7437 5708). It's very small and so definitely intimate. The tables and chairs are rickety and non matching – this isn't particularly a selling point, they just are.

Dribbly candles cast very flattering lighting (she'll appreciate that) and the food is divine. The menu changes weekly and is hand written – a nice touch. The staff are jolly helpful and will help you chose the perfect wine to suit you (unlike the waiters in *Quo Vadis* who serenely glide around on their oiled casters intimidating diners into ordering fantastically expensive wines – I pointed at a £25 bottle of wine to which the oily one tutt tutted and said he thought my guest – boyfriend of yonks thank God and so not needing to be impressed – would prefer this one and pointed to a £70 bottle! A pox on him).

Anyway, I can't remember what I ate, I just remember loving it – *Andrew Edmunds* that is. Four of us went and had starters and mains and the boys had puddings (don't they always?) and a bottle of fizz to begin with and then a shed-load of red. the bill was £50 each. If you're taking a young lady out you probably don't want to follow our lead on the amount drunk. As I said, I don't remember what I ate... Good luck.

💬 **Hels**

Andrew Edmunds on Lexington Street is a lovely, reasonably priced romantic restaurant. If you want intimate, you will get it here. The seating plan is cosy, food is hearty and tasty, wine list is good and priced across a range. Service is friendly. You might even forget you are in W1.

🗩 **Ang**

I'd recommend two things in terms of food in London. One is www.toptable.co.uk – it's great to get ideas and registering often allows you special discounts and offers for food at some of the best restaurants in London.

My choice for a 'top table' though, would be *Le Boudin Blanc* in Shepherds Bush Market. The setting is great and the food French. It's not crazily expensive for London – 80 quid for two – but the setting is fantastic. Quiet little market square with pubs all around. Opposite Green Park, so nice for walking to after a stroll in the park, and near the tube station.

🗩 **Crazy Eddy**

I have a few suggestions for Laurence about where to take a girl for her birthday. Not sure where you are based but here are some places I'd like to be taken in similar circumstances.

Smiths of Smithfields. The middle restaurant is lovely and not too expensive (compared to the top one). They have a really good menu, including a good selection of meat and fish in a really nice atmosphere. Small wooden tables, low lighting but not too much of an intimate vibe.

The Rivington Bar and Grill. Top food, good sized portions and a nice lounge area where you can sit and have another few bottles of wine after your meal. It's in the middle of Old Street and Great Eastern Street.

Cru. Really great food, and very chilled, it's lit by tea lights but still has hussle and noise from the kitchen. It's near Hoxton Square.

There's also a really nice pub in Hammersmith called the *Anglers Arms* that does the best pub grub ever and not only that but they have tonnes of blackboards filled with every choice of wine you could hope for and it's all at pub prices!

Hope that helps.

🗩 **Pesk**

For moderately cheap and good you can't do better than Upper Street. Three winners in terms of romantic but not cheesy ambience and good portions are:

Le Mercury. You could definitely do a good meal for two people for £70 here. Nice little French place, right near Almeida Theatre. Romantic ambience. Book in advance as it is popular.

Le Petit Auberge. Over the road from Mercury. Fantastically interesting menu with game and exotic fish that changes all the time.

Casale Franco. You have to keep your eyes open to spot this place – the entrance is down a back alley next to *Vultures* video shop and it shares this entrance with a car mechanic's! However, don't let this less than glamorous first impression put you off.

It is lovely inside and the food is simply outstanding. When I went I had seafood risotto and it was cracking – wine was pretty good too.

🗩 **Matthew**

For fish I would definitely recommend *Livebait*. Me and my bloke had a romantic dinner there (at the Covent Garden one) to celebrate our anniversary and after three courses and a bottle of nice and not too cheap wine and coffees and stuff it came to £80.

They source their fish ethically if you're into that sort of thing, and you can look at the amazing display they have near the kitchen. If you like shellfish they do this fantastic platter to share, with lobster and gigano prawns, and mussels, whelks, cockles – all that kind of stuff. I had the most amazing melty halibut rarebit thing when we were there. They also have a pre-theatre menu which is a steal.

The only downside for your evening of lurve is that it has a very (deliberate) canteen feel. The whole place is tiled which means when the place is full the chatter is very loud, and it's not lit particularly romantically. However, we unintentionally timed our meal from about 6.45pm until about 9pm, so the place really emptied out of the pre-theatre crowd and got quite mellow until the regular diners turned up as we were getting ready to leave. And they gave us a little table in the corner near the door which is sheltered by a partition thingy, so we did feel quite protected from the crowd. But the tables are quite packed in and it was pretty noisy in the busy periods, but the service was fine and the fish was fab.

Anyway, not sure it fits all your criteria, but worth a look. Hope it helps, enjoy your dinner!

💬 Sqweno

May I suggest *Julie's* in Notting Hill Gate? Fits all the specs you're looking for and is absolutely magic! Call and reserve a room in the Forge (or the little room at the end of it and to the left). Pictures, menus etc., are all available at their site: www.juliesrestaurant.com.

Good Luck.

💬 Garth

Le Bouchon by South Kensington station is perfect. Surprisingly cheery French hospitality, great wines, great food. Très, très romantic. Bill for two with two bottles of wine and two courses was about £75 when we went.

🖵 gizbourn

Marine Ices in Chalk Farm Road – dead good Italian food; three courses for less than 20 quid each without booze, the ice cream menu is fantabulosa, take some home to bed! And the staff are nice.

🖵 Maureen

LOVE

Can anyone give me a bit of advice here? I was wondering if anyone knew of some nice little places around Hampstead/Camden area where I could take someone out for dinner. I had completely forgotten about Valentine's Day until a mate mentioned it the other day. Furthermore, I have just moved here recently and don't know where the good/bad spots are. Not only that but for once I have someone to take out – I really should have remembered! Any tips would be much appreciated. Places which won't break the bank too badly would be cool too. Thanks a lot! And Happy Valentine's Day.

🖵 ArPF

Although more a gastropub than a restaurant, per se, my own ladyfriend was very impressed by the *Crown and Goose* on Delancey Street in Camden. It ticks all the right romantic boxes, being small and cosy, with candles on the tables, lots of dark wood, and a real fire. Particularly pleasant on a cold February evening.

🖵 Tallchap

I had a fantastic first date at a Caribbean restaurant in Camden called *The Mango Rooms*. The food was great, the cocktails even better and with lively music and colourful paintings on the walls it was a really enjoyable place to have dinner. However for me, the love of the restaurant lasted much longer than love of the man who took me there... don't know if that's a bad omen for a Valentine's Day recommendation!

💬 Em

Party time

THE PLACE

I'm organising a party for a chum and thought I would seek advice from the collective wisdom of you kind LBLers.

Want it to be intimate – I guess about fifty people there. Should be a clubby type atmosphere, just us, located centralish with perhaps a dash of south. There will be disc jockeys, who I'm pretty certain I can get for free, leaving just a venue with bar and some kind of sound system to find.

Also, somewhere where I can guide said friend in to be surprised by assembled throng – so not too many windows! How much would this be? Where should this be? Thanks.

💬 Luc

The Crypt of St Martin's in the Fields is available for hire and makes a nice setting for a party – pillars, not too many windows and lots of character. A friend of mine had his 40th there recently and it's been the scene of more than a couple of work parties. You might have to supply your own mobile disco though, as I'm not sure it has a sound system of its own.

💬 Mike

Having organised a number of events similar in the past, my experience suggests that most bars (provided they have the room) will give you a space for a limited or long-time for free if you are going to offer them fifty patrons spending money across their bar. You may even be able to negotiate a cheap beer/wine/drink of the night for your group.

Try finding a bar with an upstairs/downstairs area they can set aside. There's plenty in Clapham and surrounding area. My fave? Check out upstairs at *Firefly* (Clapham Common) or upstairs at *Jamie's* in Poland Street, Soho.

💬 **Tonytone**

A great venue for around fifty people is the private bar downstairs of the *Slug and Lettuce* (therefore no windows), St Martin's Lane, which has a good atmosphere and great furniture. We had an event there recently and there is plenty room for a DJ too.

💬 **KB**

Juno on Shoreditch High Street is a good venue. Decks, a reasonable (but not brilliant) PA, free-to-very-cheap to hire (can't quite remember), plus, if you show up with a passport to prove it's your birthday on (or near) that weekend they can apply for a 2am licence. My mate did it recently, it was a good night.

💬 **Dirtos**

I can heartily recommend *Abigail's Party* on Brewer Street in Soho. Speak to a nice man called Dan on 020 7434 2911. He sorted out a very good night for about sixty of us recently, and at no charge either.

Try the *Extra Time Sports Bar* on Long Lane, just round the corner from Barbican tube. The upstairs has room for up to about 120 people, you can hire their DJ or use your own – or just take a stash of CDs and they'll play them. You can get a late licence until 2am, plus they have big TV screens and will put on videos for you. (They're not fans of hard core porn, but we had *Bagpuss* and *Grease 2* playing throughout the night at our party, which is about as rocking as you can get, I believe).

And the best thing? It's free. Subject to minimum bar spend, anyway, but it's about £500 – pretty reasonable compared to the £2k that some of the central London bars charge. You pay £20 for every hour after 11pm, and that's it. Wonderful.

💬 **Katkins**

Try the *Doghouse* in Wardour Street opposite *Europa Foods*. A single door leads to a subterranean bar that has a good sound system and does excellent cocktails. Happy hour equals half price so £3 for a Long Island Iced Tea is all good. One of the ante-chambers should hold the required number. A well-discovered but surprisingly under-used gem. It used to be artistically graffitied inside but is a bit more mainstream now.

💬 **Andrew**

Andrew mentioned the *Doghouse* in Wardour Street as a fab venue for parties. Bowowow! My friends and I have been keeping this place our own little secret for two years now (we're not selfish, we just enjoy a good night out without the sardine factor).

The *Doghouse* is not just a great party venue, it's perfect for those pop-in-after-work-for-a-chilled-and-groovy-night times. Great little vibe in there and completely poser-free. Their 'no ties' policy says it all.

💬 **GrayArea**

Oi, will you lot stop talking about the *Doghouse*. It's about the only bearable place to get a drink in Soho, mainly cos' it doesn't get too crowded. If you tell everyone and it gets really popular, I'll have to sit on the park bench and drink Special Brew. And it'll be your fault.

💬 **Hiccup**

Vic Naylor's on St John's Street, EC1 is very nice for that kind of thing – had my 30th there a few weeks ago – they were really helpful, have decks and you can order food and have the whole place to yourself.

💬 **Ant**

A friend faced with a similar organisational pre-party headache had this website to thank for coming to his rescue: www.viewlondon.co.uk/party.asp.
   Hope your party pops.

💬 **GrayArea**

I can recommend *Play Bar* near Old Street. It's open until 4am on weekends with an option to bring your own DJs. Deposit of £150 is required, but this is returned if your minimum bar bill is £1500 or more (shouldn't be a problem if you are there until 4am). My friends hired it recently and loved it. This bar is one of a group of three, another one is the *Living Bar* in Brixton but I'm not sure where the third one is.
   Not sure if they will have availability for the date you want but they do get cancellations sometimes, so it's worth a try. Have a look at www.playbar.co.uk.

💬 **Sladey**

SASS

It's one of my best mates' 30th soon and I have been assigned the task of finding a sassy, sexy venue with lots of flirting potential where we can sip cocktails and feel Sex-and-the-City-like that evening.

Not quite sure how I have managed to give them the reputation that I am a cool chick about town, but please LBLers, could you help me out so my cover isn't blown? Location-wise I'm thinking either SW or Central. There will be about six of us and we scrub up pretty well.

🗨 Pol

For Sex-and-the-City-style cocktails my favourite destination is the *Long Bar* at the *Sanderson Hotel* (off Oxford Street) although it can be a bit too bright in there at times. Plenty of people-watching though!

Also, *Hush* is good (off Bond Street). They do plenty of great cocktails and their Cosmopolitans are divine! They also do tasty nibbles although the staff can be a bit slow on occasion. But on the plus side, they have great '30-plus lighting' and squashy sofas for when your manolos get a bit uncomfortable!

🗨 Carrie B

The *Rockwell Bar* at the *Hilton Trafalgar Square* guarantees good sass in the city. Then there's *Hakkassan* for cocktails you'll still be yabbering about the day after. Similarly, the *Long Bar* at the *Sanderson* and the *Light Bar* at *St Martin's Lane Hotel* both hit the G-lam spot.

🗨 Dumb Brunette

There's loads and loads of good cocktail bars around. In the West End, *Eagle Bar Diner* is a good place to go, not too expensive and has great DJs, atmosphere etc.

Lab Bar in Soho is also really good but arrive early as it's quite small and gets full quickly. More SW-way there is *Zander* in Victoria which boasts the longest bar in the country. They are owned by the same people as *Bank* restaurant which does make them a little pricey though. Also in Victoria is *B-Bar* which has a nice downstairs bar with lots of comfy sofas etc. Their cocktails are really good and reasonably priced. If you want to go a little more upmarket then *Zeta* in the *Hilton Mayfair* is really good, about £15 to get in and they have DJs until about 3am but again, that's a bit more on the expensive side.

Hope that's given you a few ideas, there are loads more. I could go on forever, but a good website for looking up places to go is www.london-eating.co.uk which does both restaurants and bars.

💬 **cocktail gal**

Detroit is a good, atmospheric bar off Neal Street near Covent Garden – classy music and fantastic cocktails. But for somewhere with probably more flirting potential try *Hakkassan* (8 Hanway Place, London, W1T 1HF) be warned though, dinner is very pricey but the cocktails are fairly standard.
If you really want to go for it then try the *Sanderson Hotel* – really pricey but almost more *Sex and the City* then the show itself!

💬 **David**

I highly recommend *Thirst*, in Greek Street as a place to go for cocktails. Their 'stupid hour' runs from 5–7pm with cocktails

at half price then it's happy hour til 9pm. Their list is really
good but they will also make anything you want if it's not
on there. Usually fairly laid back and relaxed until around
8.30pm and doesn't get over-run with tourists.

🖵 **LuLu**

The Heights bar on the 15th floor of *St George's Hotel*,
Langham Place W1B (close to BBC Broadcasting House)
might be a good place to start the evening.

It's been quiet the last few times I've been, so perhaps not
enough flirting opportunities for the whole night, but the
view over London is good and its penthouse chic would get
you all in the mood. Excellent toilets, which is important,
and you get free nuts.

🖵 **LizardPUB**

GARDEN PARTY

**I have a 30th birthday party looming. Can anybody
recommend a good club or late bar in the Covent
Garden/Holborn area to go to after the pub?**
**Preferably one with a largish dance floor that's full of people
who know how to get down and boogie rather than dullards
parading round with a 'look at me, I'm so cool' attitude?**

🖵 **Caroline**

Caroline, a decent place to boogie after hours in Holborn
is downstairs in the *Sway Bar* on Great Queen Street. It's got
a big dance floor, as well as a big comfy seating area, and
it has a good mix of both pretentious tossers, and normal
people out for a good time.

🖵 **Gizzard**

Try *The Gardening Club* for your birthday, right in Covent Garden. Always had a great time whenever I've been there. Plus you can usually email them if there's a big group and get on the guest list for guaranteed entry.

It also has the benefit of not being full of 18-year-olds too pissed to stand up.

💬 Steve

WHERERLOO?

Where are the good pubs in Waterloo? Not silly, trendy, 'long benches with loud music and too crowded' type places. Like that awful *Fire Station* thingy we ended up in last time.

A bit of atmosphere, decent beer and not more then ten minutes from the station is what we're talking about here.

💬 El Presidente

If you walk down to Lower Marsh Street there is a wicked pub on the corner (Westminster Bridge Road) called *The Walrus Social*. Upstairs (not so well known) are loads of big sofas. Very relaxing, and they do good food too.

💬 platinumdan

Auberge on Sandell Street is worth trying, or a little further, but still only three minutes walk, is *The King's Arms* on Roupell Street. It serves proper beer and does great Thai food. Big room in the back usually means there are seats too.

💬 Robram

A great pub in Waterloo is The Stage Door. It's behind the *Old Vic* theatre on the corner of Webber and Gray Streets.

It's a proper pub, decently done out, good range of drinks and food served. It's run by an Aussie couple who are brilliant and the bar staff are always lovely too.

I found it due to work location but it is a favourite meeting/drinking place with all of my friends.

⌐▢ **Big Sis**

Waterloo is bad for pubs, El Presidente, and believe me it gets a lot worse than the *Fire Station* which I would regard as one of the better ones. Try the *Anchor & Hope*, 36 The Cut, for a more traditional feel.

⌐▢ **Spammed**

You should try the *Anchor & Hope* on The Cut, about ten minutes from Waterloo and along towards Southwark tube. Formerly *Bar Citrus*, I used to spend happy Sunday mornings there while my pants happily spun around in soapy bliss in the nearby Laundromat; back then the coffee was excellent and the drinks menu bizarre.

Nowadays, (as I found out only recently, not while doing any washing, but instead out of an evening re-visiting my old haunts), its much darker and groovier. Half of it is now a bar, and the other half a candle-lit restaurant, where you seem to be able to just drop in, and where I remember ordering Teal if because I remembered it was as small duck and at the time this seemed vastly amusing. My friend had the cod, also very nice.

Not the largest of places, but nicely chilled and with an unusual menu to choose from.

⌐▢ **costumekitten**

There are some good pubs near Waterloo – two to recommend are:

The Hole in the Wall – opposite the main steps to Waterloo – it's got a reasonable juker and serves decent beer. Also, being under the trains lines going to Waterloo East, it makes for interesting vibrations.

The King's Arms – Nice pub, about five minutes walk away. Near that place in Grand Designs, you know, where they spent gazillions on then got into a dispute with the neighbours over planning permission.)

Be good though, and treat them nice. They're lovely.

💬 **Dave**

My favourite unpretentious boozer round there is *The Hole In The Wall*, opposite the main entrance to the station and underneath train tracks. It's a basic, non-refurbished pub with a small room and a bigger one, good beers, and an occasional earthquake from the trains passing overhead.

💬 **B-)**

KARAOKE

My mate is having a hen night in London and she likes a bit of Karaoke when she's had a few, so I wanted to book somewhere that allowed us to get there around 11pm and then sing until the small hours, but I can't find anything suitable. Any ideas?

💬 **Atobagofan**

Karaoke Box, 18 Frith Street Soho, 020 7494 3878 – a great place for late hours Karaoke – open until 3am I think. They charge around £35 for a 10-person room, so per person it's not too expensive, and you get tambourines to play with too!

Karaoke heaven! (Make sure you book in advance though as it's very popular around closing time.)

☐ **Little Miss B**

The best place for late night karaoke is *Karaoke Box* on Frith Street. It's pretty much opposite *Ronnie Scott's* and identifiable only by the Japanese writing outside and the 'Closed' sign on the door (that means it's open, but you have to book ahead on a Saturday). You hire a room for your group and the play list contains all the soft rock classics and power ballads you could wish for...

☐ **Prenders**

We recently did this very thing – hired a room downstairs in a Korean restaurant and sang until the early hours. The place is called *Assa*, 53 St Giles High Street (near Tottenham Court Road, back of Centre Point). We paid 30 quid an hour for the largest room but there are smaller rooms too. The food is ace, but watch out for the price of the drinks – Jacob's Creek at 25 quid a bottle. We negotiated down to 12 but he told us to keep it a secret (just between us LBLers then).

☐ **Miss Lake**

For a great cheap eat, try *Misato* on Wardour Street, for huge portions of Japanese food.

☐ **Little G**

And finally

PAVEMENT

It isn't summer and we don't live in France. So stop huddling outside bars with your cold beers and cold cigarettes pretending we do. Half a glimpse of the sun and we think: 'yay! Café culture! wipe the rain off your seat and never mind the fag ash blowing in your gob! this is summer!' Well stop it. Look at yourself. Your fingers are stiff and blue, and back inside the pub the heating is still on. Go inside, you idiot.

⌐ Jess

I've just returned from Spain having witnessed, in torrential rain, the Spanish drinking coffees and beer (not mixed together, well I assume not anyway) outside pavement cafés with umbrellas up.

Each drinker had an umbrella and all drinkers had a look of 'this is completely normal' upon their face. Us (sensible?) English were inside, warm and toasty getting rat-arsed on cheap Sangria.

It's Europe-wide this idiot stuff.

⌐ Miss Lake

Entertainment

They say that all work and no play makes Jack a dull boy. And whoever they are, they're right. Fortunately London is packed to the gills with things to do with your non-work time – from pub quizzes and tap dancing to free jazz in the park and beach parties by the Thames. In this section you'll not only find the best places to enjoy all of the 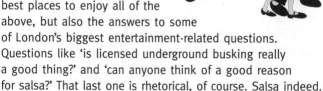 above, but also the answers to some of London's biggest entertainment-related questions. Questions like 'is licensed underground busking really a good thing?' and 'can anyone think of a good reason for salsa?' That last one is rhetorical, of course. Salsa indeed.

The games people play

QUIZ

I know quiz nights sound a tad nerdy, but I haven't really found many good ones in the Smoke. By good ones, I don't mean the rubbish 20 general knowledge type quizzes that you find in certain pubs. I'm talking about ones that have perhaps four, five and often many more rounds, that are difficult to an extent that you may know some of the questions, but you don't just sit there going 'what the fuck?' and that you want to go back to week in and week out.

Preferably South London, if anyone knows one that fits this bill.

💬 Robram

The Cedar Tree on Putney Bridge Road does a pleasingly frustrating quiz on Sunday night, 9pm. It's only thirty questions, with rounds of five covering sport, pictures, music, trivia etc, and it's fiendish. Prizes are cash and beer, and there's a rarely claimed and frequently enormous rolling jackpot for scores above a set target. First night I was there a team walked off with over £700. It fills up fast when the jackpot's large. Get there by eight for a table.

💬 Rastaban

I have been doing a pub quiz for the last few months based in *The Latchmere* pub on Battersea Park Road, Tuesdays at 9pm. It is run by a strange, harmless, semi-lunatic, is quite tough and has a very good, regular attendance.

There are three basic rounds, which consist of either two or three sets of five questions on the 'normal' topics (each question scoring a point). Each round also includes a 'quizling'.

The quizling consists of three questions (each scoring a point), the answers to which have a theme (which scores two points). The final part of each round is the 'beer' question which scores no points but the prize for winning is a round of (four) drinks.

The beer questions are along the lines of:

Q. What is the length in km of the Gota Canal in Sweden?

Q. According to the CIA factbook, what is the current population of Belgium?

Nearest answer wins.

Occasionally, there is an overlaying quiz. Recent examples have included, 'name the face', 'match the quote to the person' and 'numbers code', i.e. the 7 D of C is the 7 Days of Christmas.

The difficulty of the quiz varies but it is one of the hardest/most varied I have ever attempted.

💬 DT

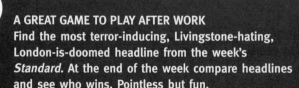

A GREAT GAME TO PLAY AFTER WORK
Find the most terror-inducing, Livingstone-hating, London-is-doomed headline from the week's *Standard*. At the end of the week compare headlines and see who wins. Pointless but fun.

Previous winning headlines include:

'TONIGHT WE BOMB!'

'LIVINGSTONE – AL QAEDA LINK!'

'CONGESTION – WE'RE ALL GOING TO DIE!'

💬 Con

If you want a good quality pub quiz I can recommend the
Elephant Inn on Ballards Lane, North Finchley (next to
Waitrose). It's not South London I'm afraid – nearest tube
West Finchley – but it's well worth travelling for. It's on
Monday nights at 9pm and is written by a guy who does
crosswords for the *Guardian*, apparently.

There are five rounds, each with a theme. If you guess
the theme then you can use it to work out some of the
answers you're not sure about, so you don't have to be
quite such an expert in trivia as for other quizzes. There are
also bonus rounds and five-in-a-rows to make it more
interesting and – best of all – a snowball round (separate
to the main quiz) that I won £125 on not so long ago. And
if that hasn't sold it to you they also do excellent Thai food.
What more could you want?

🗩 **Sleepy Tim**

I know it's not south, but *The Elgin* on Ladbroke Grove has
a wicked quiz. It has loads of different rounds using a
multitude of media – the 'what film are these stills taken
from' and 'name this really obscure track in thirty seconds'
were particular favourites – and is presented by a man who's
dishy in a Face from *A-Team* way and funny like DLT.

And you get to win booze which, in a pub, cannot be
sniffed at. It's on Sunday nights at 6pm and you'll see me
in the corner in the tatty anorak, stroking my hair in a
suggestive/coy manner. And of course, looking smug when
I come first (again) and claim my bottle of sherry.

🗩 **Lulabelle**

There is a Quiz League of London – www.qll.org.uk – which is a team quiz; individuals answer their own question which is thrown open to their team if they don't know it, or to the opposition if it is answered incorrectly.

The standard in Division One is blinding (there are numerous champions of Mastermind, Brain of Britain, 15–1 and University Challenge on various of the teams), but there are plenty of other average-to-good quizzers.

For a city the size of London, it's surprising that there are only 20 or so teams... I'm sure a few more wouldn't be turned away.

💬 loaf

DRINKING, GAMES

I'm looking for a pub to fulfil a specific purpose, namely being suitable for game playing. Not having done so since I were a mere lad, I've developed a sudden hankering to play board games that take hours, for example *Risk* or *Diplomacy*. I particularly want to do this with my friends on autumn/winter weekend days in a pleasant pub environment.

What I'm looking for is somewhere that – between maybe 1 and 8pm – is quiet, preferably with a fire, no distractions of television, loud music or boisterous youths and an enlightened attitude towards people who aren't quite as geeky as their activities may appear, honest. Preferably accessible from South London but can travel.

💬 Laurence

In response to the search for a quality pub with board games I can highly recommend *The Dove*, 24 Broadway Market (corner of Broadway Market and Duncan Road), E8.

Great food, great atmosphere and the largest selection of beers known to man to accompany your gaming pleasure.

🖵 **Pubster**

I too have recently hankered after the games of youth. Anyone for *Axis and Allies* etc?

Only problem you might have would be some old gaming laws. Can't think what they are now but I do know that some over-officious barman has stopped us playing poker for matches before. *Duke of Edinburgh* in Brixton would be great for this though.

🖵 **Bobbuilder**

The Dean Swift Pub, near Shad Thames on the south side of the river, right next to Tower Bridge is ideal. They even have a few of their own board games scattered around the pub for people to play (*Jenga* etc.)

I used to spend lunchtimes in there when I worked near Tower Bridge, their lasagne being a particular favorite of mine.

It's quite small and cosy, but also has big tables, ideal for *Risk* or the like.

🖵 **Jack**

This probably doesn't help Laurence since it's all a bit far from South London, but *Rose's Ale House* in Highgate (on Archway Road) and the *Larrik* in Finsbury Park (on Stroud Green Road) are both pubs with a supply of board games, space to play them in, and a fire.

🖵 **Billy**

I have spent many a happy Wednesday evening shaking my tiddlywinks at *The Double Six Club*, otherwise known as the board game night at *The Office* (3–5 Rathbone Place, W1). Highly recommended.

 Jacquelyn

I think I've invented a new game to while away your working hours with. The aim is to combine the plots of three films into one paragraph.

For example:
Boogie Nights x *Taxi Driver* x *Free Willy*

In which a massively endowed, hung like a whale, psychotic, Vietnam vet taxi driver working the graveyard shift also moonlights as a adult performer but finds that after indulging in too much nasal stimulation he can no longer retrieve his manhood from his boxers. Saddened by his plight, local kids band together and try to encourage the community to help. This results in a wonderfully life-affirming bit of social bonding. But just at the moment where it looks like he'll finally be free of his pants he becomes paranoid because people are looking at him (You lookin' at me? There's nobody else here... etc.,) while he stands in front of his mirror, so he shaves his head into a mohican and shoots every-one. It could be called *Free the Night Driver's Willy*.

auawsha

There is a Quiz League of London – www.qll.org.uk – which is a team quiz; individuals answer their own question which is thrown open to their team if they don't know it, or to the opposition if it is answered incorrectly.

The standard in Division One is blinding (there are numerous champions of Mastermind, Brain of Britain, 15–1 and University Challenge on various of the teams), but there are plenty of other average-to-good quizzers.

For a city the size of London, it's surprising that there are only 20 or so teams... I'm sure a few more wouldn't be turned away.

💬 loaf

POT

I've noticed that the number of pool tables in London seems to have dwindled recently, leaving only the monster rip-offs like *Elbow Rooms* and their shiny clones. Does anybody know of any good places that are reasonably quiet, have a couple of tables and charge per game? Anywhere within zone 1/2 really, I'm getting an itchy pool arm.

💬 lanem

You are quite right; places where you can get that right arm action flowing are becoming rarer every day. I imagine it is something to do with a table taking up floor space and London bars increasingly wanting to cram more people in but the tables are there – if you look hard enough.

The Duchy in Kennington has a very good table that costs 80p (and doesn't require the right change) on the corner of Cardigan Street and Sancroft Street, SE11. As long as you can live with the local teenagers who often frequent (slightly chavish but not at all rough and quite a good laugh when you play winner stays on), then I can highly recommend it.

For those that play with both cues, or indeed another cue entirely, there is a pub called *The Little Apple* (or the something Apple, I'm not entirely sure) who have a good but, rather appropriately, bent table costing just 70p. Also in Kennington on the east end of Kennington Lane and the corner of Renfrew Road, it is also highly recommendable, even if you are as straight as long red from Ronnie O'Sullivan.

Finally, in Kennington there is *The Pilgrim* next to the *Tesco* on Kennington Lane, again quite good and fairly cheap (80p or £1 I think). Not the friendliest of pub atmospheres due to the layout more than anything but not awful.

In Clapham Common there is a pub, the name escapes me, on the corner of Cresset Street and Stonehouse Street which has a table (about £1 I think) but I've not been in there for a while. *The Manor Arms* on the next corner has no table but I believe it to be one of the finest pubs anywhere.

For the more serious, *Rileys Snooker Hall* has lots of tables and there's one just next to *Inigo* (bar) on Wandsworth Road (by the junction with Cedars Road). You pay by the hour rather than the game and last time I was there it was fairly reasonable, although on busy nights you may have to wait for a table. The word on the street is that there is a hall in Brixton too but I have not been there, don't know where it is and it may not even be a *Rileys*.

The only one I know of in Central London is a pub near Green Park tube. It's been an age since I've been but I think it might be *The Half Moon* and is possibly on Half Moon Street, off Piccadilly. Failing that it'll be on one of the next roads along, off Piccadilly and may be called something entirely different but there is a pub there or thereabouts that has two or three tables upstairs.

Apart from that, I'm not aware of many more. I'm sure there are but you do have to seek them out. The Hampshire Hog between Hammersmith and Chiswick used to have one (whether it still does or not I don't know), The *Famous Three Kings* has a few (next to West Kensington tube station) but I have boycotted it since it became a 'Sports bar' and they ripped up the sticky carpet. If you walk from there down North End Road to Fulham there are a few but the pubs aren't that great and for North and East London I will leave you in the capable hands of someone else.

💬 **Kenning Tom**

I could recommend my lovely local and its pool table but then I'd never get a game on a Friday night would I? And I get enough grief from the lads there taking the piss out of a girl playing pool (it's the East End dontchaknow) so I recommend looking on pub website www.beerintheevening.com which is fantastic for finding pubs in any area and you can select your requirements e.g. beer garden/food/live music or indeed, pool table.

💬 **Bealos**

Not that I want the place completely overrun on what is my quiet Tuesday night, but the *Progress Bar* on Tufnell Park Road has free pool on Tuesday nights on proper American pool tables.

💬 **Tim**

An open secret, but opposite *Elbow Rooms* in Shoreditch is *The Pool Bar* which has free pool all day on Sundays as long as you get a drink in every now and then. No booking system so take your chances.

💬 Gavin

If you want a decent quiet game of pool, try the *Wilmington Arms* on Rosebery Avenue, EC1, just up from Mount Pleasant Sorting Office. Usually pretty quiet, because it's an old-school pub in a sea of trendiness, and it has two decent sized tables at the back. I'm not saying they'll be empty, but they're nicer than most other places I've been.

💬 robram

In a world where there seems to be no respite from the ongoing atrocities of, erm, almost everyone I can think of, there needs to be an escape.

Here it is: go out and buy *'Live: The Up In Smoke Tour'* on video. Watch it on Sunday while *Songs of Praise* is on. Flick between the video channel and BBC1 at intervals of ten seconds. The juxtaposition of angelic children singing in beautiful contralto about the eternal greatness of God and Snoop Dee-Oh-Double-Gee mumbling about 'sticky-icky-icky' as Dr Dre and Nate Dogg ride around the stage on platinum-plated tricycles and Eminem abuses a customised blow-up doll will keep you intellectually amused for hours while demonstrating the rich and varied tapestry of the modern world.

It's good to exercise the mind, once in a while.

💬 Wishbone

Try upstairs at the *Black Horse* on Rathbone Place. They've got about eight tables and it's not massively expensive either.

💬 **Looska**

Loads of pubs in and off Fleet Street have pool tables. They are rarely in use very late as the area is in that is it City/isn't it City, where there's no residents but the pubs stay open.

💬 **Neil LeM**

Try *Snooker Lovers* in Dalston (Kingsland Road between Crossway and Barrets Road). It looks frightening from the outside. You have to buzz in and go down a long corridor, to apparent certain death, but once there the welcome is warm, if a little perplexed if you're not Turkish or Chinese. You can play snooker for three hours (this normally gives me time to play best of one frame) and drink lots of Efes beer and leave with change from 10 quid.

💬 **Snooker loopy**

Shelley's Pub at 10 Stafford Street, just off Piccadilly has three tables in the basement at about £2 a pop.

💬 **Bel**

PUTT

I used to take great pleasure in wandering around a pitch and putt course with some friends, idly whacking the ball about and caring for nothing more than being out in the open air. Since moving to London, however, I have failed entirely to find a nice place to do this. I don't want to play serious golf, I just want long enough holes to warrant my rather energetic style of driving, situated in a park where I'm not likely to have my golf balls nicked by the local youth.

Can anyone help?

🗨 Ted

There's a decent pitch and putt course on the hill just below Alexandra Palace – it's a quality place to spend a couple of hungover hours on a Sunday, reasonably long holes and enough foliage to keep things interesting if you spoon it.

🗨 **Andyandy**

If you're looking for a nice place to play pitch and putt, you should give Queen's Park a go. You can have a nice relaxing game without fear of getting your balls nicked and there's also a nice café there – and tennis courts if you're feeling particularly energetic.

🗨 **Cinders4**

There's a great pitch and putt course in Queens Park NW6. Beautifully surrounded with huge oak trees and picturesque gardens – it even sports a gazebo featuring swing bands during some summer weekends.

The course itself it a nine-hole, three par. They supply you
with two balls, a nine iron and a putter for about 'fore' quid.
See you at the tees.

💬 **Brad Finley**

Music

JUKE

What are the best pub jukeboxes in the capital?

💬 **Linda Palermo**

Check out *The Social* in Islington. It has what's called the
'heavenly jukebox', which has some great music – both older
classics and the newer stuff. To see if it's your style check
out the websites www.heavenly100.com or www.thesocial.com.
I promise you – you won't be disappointed.

💬 **DEBSFROMN1**

The one in the *Shakespeare* in Stoke Newington is free,
which is always good unless you're the kind of hopeless
drunk who puts money in it anyway (me). Not a bad selection of music either. But my favourites are both the old-fashioned kind with the little records behind the glass screen
– one to be found in The Three Kings on Clerkenwell Green
(a fine hostelry, even without its juke box) and the other
in a tiny wee bar just off Oxford Street whose name escapes
me presently but that's good because I want to keep it
a secret. Gen-u-wine old-fashioned good stuff.

💬 **Magpie**

The Griffin in Hoxton/Shoreditch, near Curtain Road I think, has a great jukebox. And the Polish bar opposite is fab too.

🗩 **slayer73**

Oooh I do believe the *Salisbury Hotel* on Green Lanes, North London may have one of the best jukeboxes in the capital. Absolutely fantastic pub where you can always guarantee hearing Pixies, Blondie, and at least one track off *Screamadelica*. Beautiful, friendly pub with excellent Czech beer and a warm atmosphere! Yay!

🗩 **Jean**

SPIN

I want to become a DJ. It can't be hard. I mean, real idiots do it. Will someone teach me?

🗩 **Suzanne**

A couple of mates and I had the same attitude. Having talked about putting a night on for years, we're doing the first one this week. None of us can DJ properly. We just emailed a hipster bar and asked if we could do a night. They said yes. I intend to (*gasp*) play one ace record after another for an hour or so. Easy. Like a lot of things in life, DJing is a confidence trick, i.e., anyone can do it if they are confident enough.

🗩 **Richard**

Let's imagine that you already have access to, or bought yourself two decks (and I should recommend that anyone entering into DJing should invest in a decent set of decks, Technics 1210s/1200s are still industry standard, and are approximately £350 a deck plus mixer, with EQs which are a very good idea, at least £100–£150) and a set of headphones. Then you need some records, which average about £5 a go. Twenty records would be a good number to start off with – but be warned vinyl addiction is a fairly common complaint amongst DJs. So now you have the equipment, how do you actually DJ?

Well the simple answer is that you listen to the tune that is playing in one ear, and the other record that is not playing to the unsuspecting public in the headphones. Then all you have to do is count the beats. You have the match up the first, second, third, and fourth beat of a bar. Once they are in line, you can do a smooth mix between the two records, using the EQs on the mixer to make it sound better. Simple hey?

Well not quite, as people listen with two ears, not one, so you have to get over the fact that you are listening to one thing with one ear and another thing with another ear. I have met one person, a Metallica fan of all things, who managed to learn in under an hour, but then again he had been playing in a band for 15 years and had an intrinsic understanding of music. I have also heard of people who have taken six months to learn. Most people take about two months to learn to DJ. You might want to bear in mind that by the time you see these 'idiots' DJing out, that they have done the hard graft in learning to beat match. Then all you have to do is learn how to construct a set and develop your sound, which can take far longer.

Of course that is all the easy part. Then you have to blag promoters to take a risk and book you to DJ. Good luck.

Idiots? Behave...

⌐ **Fergus**

VINYL

Does anyone know anywhere to buy vinyl (you know, old-fashioned record thingies), but with a broad range of musical styles rather than just faceless techno,reggae/roots/ragga or kitsch records from the 50s (all of which I like, I hasten to add, it would just be nice to find a bit of diversity without having to go shop-hopping)?

🗨 **Pockettiger**

My favourite shop for old vinyl is *On The Beat* on Hanway Street W1, where you can find pretty much everything; punk, new wave, acid house, 60s stuff, hip hop, dodgy prog rock, old crooners. It's not the cheapest record shop in London, but it's one of the most endearing.

🗨 **Richard**

Cheapo Cheapo records, on Rupert Street (by the market bit, just down from the *Raymond Review Bar*, oh come on, don't be shy, you know where that is...) sells vinyl. Stacks of it. Literally stacks of it. So finding something you're actually after can be a bit of a pain. But it is cheap (ish). Then, of course there's *Beanos* in Croydon. Very large and very good second-hand vinyl (and other bits) store. But that's not really London, is it?

🗨 **Adam**

You should get on a train to Weston-super-Mare. The charity shops there are incredibly good – full of weird and wonderful stuff, not just records. It's because it's got such a high death rate (if anything, it's got more retirement homes than

Cromer). I once bought a plastic card shuffler in Weston. It hasn't worked since the day I got it, but it looks great.

🗨 **Kev**

FAN

Anyone know the skinny old busker in the woolly hat and weird glasses who plays on St John's road in Clapham (opposite _M&S_)? He plays the guitar, sings and has been stood there in the same spot practically every day since I moved to the area almost two years ago.

He's there all day, every day. The reason I ask is that, unlike most buskers in this city, he is dreadful. Really, truly dreadful. His music is unspeakably bad and his voice awful. It's becoming unbearable. I hear the same set from my bedroom window every day because he plays the same set every day. He has never received one penny from me ever and I have never seen anybody else give him money.

Nor have I ever seen any money sitting in his guitar case. Yet there he is. Rain or shine. Our own local minstrel. Why does he do it?! Recently a young wannabe has taken up residence in the exact same spot, only this kid has a different (and some might say unique) route to success from other buskers. Oh yes. This guy turns up at 10pm! That's right. This genius, who unlike the resident busker, can actually play well has chosen to sell his talents to a cynical and unimpressed London population at 10pm on an empty shopping street with no pubs, bars or restaurants. I swear. Now I'm no busking expert but it seems to me that optimum busking conditions would require an audience to be (A) within ear-shot and (B) awake in order to recoup some money and justify the time, effort and investment made.

This guy has avoided both. Completely. What a genius.
So, there you have it. Two buskers. One sucks, the other
plays 10pm–Midnight on weekdays. Explanations, theories
and sympathies please. Thanks.

 Avid Fan

FUN THINGS TO DO IN THE SUNSHINE...

Bookcrossing
www.bookcrossing.com/hunt/3

Flashmobbing
www.geocities.com/londonmobs

Geocaching
www.geocaching.com/map/uk.asp?lat=&lon

Letterboxing
www.spacehijackers.co.uk/letterboxing

Waterpistol Manhunt
www.dampassassins.net

 Anonymous

BUSK

Does anyone else think the licensed busking points around various London Underground stations, which are sponsored by a popular lager, completely miss the point of busking?

I used to enjoy walking through the tunnel between the Piccadilly and Victoria lines at Green Park and hearing a guy with an electric guitar playing sleazy, dirty blues, or coming down the stairs at Old Street to hear a guy with dreads and an acoustic playing Bob Marley songs.

But now, to busk at the licensed points on the underground, you apparently have to go and audition, and then sign up on a rota each week.

This has led to a huge dive in quality – it's now only the safe, polished performers that get to play, and not the more raw, exciting players that used to appear.

And besides, the idea of 'licensed' and 'sponsored' busking leaves me with a sour taste in the mouth.

💬 Stu

I was on the Executive Committee and the London District Council of the Musicians' Union when the whole buskers on the underground thing was negotiated and looked into. It was decided that in order to protect musicians who busk from the nasties who try to nick their earnings or needlessly assault them, setting up properly organised busking spots would ensure their safety. It would also regulate their time slots so that a range of musicians can play and not just those who got the spot early and also ensured a certain amount of quality. I think it's brilliant.

I'm a (female) musician and lucky that I don't have to busk in order to make a buck and I'm not so bothered about the style of music played by these people. I'm just glad that live music is somewhere in London and open to all whether they choose to contribute or not. Frankly, people should pay for music, but being as most folk think that musicians will do it for nothing as they just love playing, here we are giving you what you want! Pay, don't pay, it's up to you. If you want to hear a different kind of music, you could try making it yourself (if you want a job doing etc.) or go to a gig where its being played and pay the musicians a living wage for the privilege.

 trombonegirl

Did anyone see that sexy busker on the tube last weekend, strumming away on his guitar first in Victoria (Central line tunnel at Oxford Circus) on Friday night then on Saturday afternoon at the entrance of Tottenham Court Road? He'd put up signs saying 'SMILE!!' and 'WOW THIS BUSKER IS GOOD!' which suggests he may be American – bless. Very sexy though with sparkly blue eyes and a wee blonde goatee. Enough to make me weak at the knees anyway! So much so that I didn't even manage to throw a coin his way. If anyone knows him, tell him to come play a few songs at Bethnal Green tube!

Bellini

Indeed Stu, those licensed busk stops have managed to make music boring. When you're heading for the Jubilee line at Bond Street, we used to enjoy the dulcet tones of a man dressed in a Sylvester the Cat costume playing barmy Armstrong hits with his rubbish trumpet. The nearest thing to that concept I can find nowadays is a chubby, middle-class-looking kind of bloke having a bad bash at classical classics with his french horn at London Bridge. Sigh. Not one of them looks like they smoke tobacco, let alone crack.

💬 **BillyGoat**

I would like to thank Carling for sponsoring the busking on the underground. This is not because the quality has increased particularly but because it seems to have been the death knell for one particular 'musician'.

She used to stand near the top of the Central line stairs at Oxford Circus. She looked like something from an Aphex Twin video and squawked her way through a series of her own compositions that sounded like Aphex Twin B-Sides. This all with the accompaniment of her dreadfully out of tune guitar with strings baggier than Uncle Albert's vest. I often felt like throwing a little money in her direction but unfortunately aiming at the face is frowned upon.

So thank you Carling, thank you for getting rid of the Rat Woman of Oxford Circus.

💬 **Neuman**

JAZZ

I was skating in Battersea Park on a Tuesday evening and came across a live jazz session at the lake. We're not talking full-on jazz, just mellow, funky stuff. It was well attended with a fantastic atmosphere. These jazz sessions happen on Tuesday and Friday evenings when the weather is good. I returned on the Friday with friends in tow, picnic food, a couple of bottles of good red and a blanket. We chilled on the decking on the lake's edge and had a great evening.

It's at times like these that I love living in London.

💬 GrayArea

I too was at the jazz in the park, which was great fun and highly recommended. However, make sure you keep your eye on your bike or some scrotty little spotty, teenage bastard will steal your saddle and try and steal your front wheel. Thanks tosspot, the saddle won't fit your plastic BMX and it cost me over £50 to replace.

💬 DT

MORE JAZZ

Anyone know any good venues playing live jazz? Not big name gigs, just resident or semi-pro bands. Somewhere nice and relaxing, not pretentious. Sort of place full of smoke and a singer who sounds like they've swallowed razor blades.

Tables with candles and fifty different whiskeys. Damned if I know where such places are, but I know they're there.

💬 Daddio

Before I moved overseas I used to be a regular at the *606 Club* in Lots Road, Chelsea. It's a smoky basement venue with great food and live jazz every night. You can hear both established artists on the London jazz scene and up and coming musicians from the various music colleges. For more information visit their website at www.606club.co.uk.

⌐ Jamella

As a jazz musician's wife, I am duty-bound to say that there are not enough decent jazz venues for up-and-coming bands in London. However, I do know of a couple. *Spitz* in Spitalfields Market has a very good bebop house band that was playing regularly last year. However, the booking policy at *Spitz* has been a bit funny recently, so check the site: www.spitz.co.uk.

The Jazz Café in Camden has some interesting new band nights, but I think a toilet has more atmosphere, to be honest. There are a couple of jazz restaurants in the Camden/ Islington area, doing basement bebop the old-fashioned way. I remember one near Highbury and Islington tube, but I can't for the life of me remember the name.

The *333 Bar* in Old Street does jazz on the odd Sunday afternoon. Spouse's band (Horizon22) did a good gig there a few months ago. It's very relaxed with big sofas, nice beer and a Thai kitchen.

There is a place called *Jazz After Dark* in Soho, but I've never seen any bands there and the food is horrid. Further north is the *Vortex* in Stoke Newington: wholesome food, lots of free-jazz noodling from the likes of Billy Jenkins and Django Bates. South of the river, you've got a few pubs, such as the *Trafalgar Tavern* in Greenwich. Nice food, riverside location, mixed crowd and often a small quartet of Trinity music studes noodling in a corner. *The Crypt* at St Giles

Church in Camberwell hosts a jazz club every Friday night –
but it can get smoky. And *Funky Munky* across the street does
regular jazz DJs, plus the odd live band.

There's a weird little hotel in Greenwich, called the *White
Swan*, that has all kinds of happenings, including regular
H22 gigs (plug, plug – we've got a baby on the way – he
needs the work). It's worth checking out, if only for
the idiosyncratic decor.

💬 **Sladey**

The *100 Club* (100 Oxford Street) does Friday lunchtime
sessions that I would recommend to any jazz fan. They tend
to be mainly trad (which I love) but you will get others.
It's been a while since I've been (not working that way now)
but I assume they're still going.

💬 **Drew**

Locked out one day and waiting for house-mate to return,
I went for a couple of cheekies in the *Rose and Crown*,
just by St Mary's church, South Ealing. As I'm sat there reading
my *Standard*, some really quite nice jazz starts up.

There's a big guy in a Hawaiian shirt on drums, a 50ish
woman on bass, and an old chap called 'The Professor'
on keyboard. Now that's jazz! There were a few women sat
around, and each got up and sang a couple of standards,
including some grey haired old dear who, if you had your
eyes closed... well, let's just say she didn't sing like she
looked. The odd thing was, there couldn't have been more
than 20 people in the pub, and only half of them looked
as if they were there for the music. Anyway, according to
the barmaid, this happens on the first Monday of the month,
and starts about 8pm.

💬 **JazzMag**

MUSOS

Does anyone know any places to go to meet people who make music? I have just arrived in this town (which, it turns out, is quite big) and haven't a clue where to go to find a band (I'm a singer) or even the potential constituent parts of one.

I am not looking to join a boy band and have my 15 seconds of fame, just to meet some people who might be interested in a knockaround every now and then and maybe even a gig or two... a little help please?

GoldenEyes

I agree GoldenEyes; there must be a number of places in this town (or failing that, online) where musicians get together to meet and/or enjoy each others talents.

From what I can gather, the live music scene in London would appear to be improving slightly, but is still a far cry from what it was before it crashed in the 80s. At least places like the *Half Moon* in Putney are still going (live music every night).

I too am not interested in chasing the increasingly unattainable record-contract dream, or giving up the day-job for that matter, but would rather just get my kicks playing some decent tunes to an appreciative audience from time to time, or team up with a prodigiously talented songwriter.

So if anyone can suggest venues or resources for music lovers and musos who want to, um, get it together so to speak, then that would be, like, really cool.

Nick the Greek

There's always blues jams going on in London. *The Crown and Two Chairmen* on Dean Street, W1, do one every other Saturday. You also get to listen to ol' time before you join in.

📃 **Ian**

Goldeneyes, if you're looking for a band or other musicians, go up to Denmark Street, off Charing Cross Road. There you will find a street full of instrument shops, many of which contain musicians notice boards.

You could also have a look in the music section of *LOOT*. You'll find plenty of people, either way.

📃 **Declan**

A good website to meet and chat to other like-minded musicians/music appreciators is the forum at Resonance FM's website: www.resonanceforum.co.uk. It has info from people wanting to meet others to jam to bizarre and experimental gigs.

📃 **Bealos**

Well, a small group of musicians is starting to form with the aim of meeting up once a month for a few drinks, getting to know each other and from there, maybe jamming or forming groups together. It is all very informal at the moment so drop by the next gathering and have a couple of pints, www.londonmusiciansclub.com.

📃 **llama**

There's a fantastic venue in South-West London where I've been a regular since I moved to this country. It's called *The Grey Horse* (www.grey-horse.co.uk); check out their extremely plain site for details on their jam sessions. Just bring your instrument, and arrive early enough to put your name down to play. There's usually a fair few drummers wanting to play but other musos should be fine.

🗩 **Dan**

Don't all band types hang out at the *Barfly* in Camden all the time? Also, *The Windmill* in Brixton, despite having two scary dogs and a frightening council estate on its roof, offers all sorts of live music and is cheap and good for a laugh. Vic Godard and Subway Sect played a rare gig there a while back so it can't be too bad.

🗩 **Tiddles**

DRUM

Does anyone know of any clubs (presumably D&B) in London that encourage you to bring your own percussion along?
I've been to several squats and raves and there's always been a group of djembes and daboukas in the corner, but I'd like something a bit more dependable with less illegal smoke in the air.

🗩 **Integer Spin**

I know one club that allows and encourages drummers – it's Whirlygig, held monthly at Camden Town Hall in King's Cross. Find more info at: www.whirl-y-gig.org.uk.
The music is trancey rather than D&B.

🗩 **Tigger**

Try out *The Fridge* in Brixton.

🗩 **Pasty**

LIVE

Are there any venues in central London where you can see great live music for free? I went to a place in Brick Lane a little while ago, where they had a real variety of tunes and even a tap dancer, but wondered if there was somewhere similar which is a bit easier to get to for someone living at the west end of the Central line?

Haunted by Keane

There is so much talent around and it's great going to see live music from all kinds of people at open mic sessions where anyone can get up and share their music. Check out *Viva Viva* in Hornsey and several other places. Anyone know of good open mic nights, let me know – I may even get my guitar out and play some new stuff.

jen

Sensible Sundays on (you guessed it) Sunday at *Nambuca*, Holloway Road has been known to be a lot of fun...

greengo

A great open mic night in East London (often uses the *Rhythm Factory* and *Spitz* as venues) is Raison D'Etre. They have a website (www.reason2b.net) and an email list. Look out for Charlie Winston – fantastic!

Little G

Parties

DRESS

I'm going to a party where I have to disguise myself as an underground station. Anyone got any notions/concepts/ideas? Best suggestion so far is to buy a tall wig and go as **High Barnet**, though **Surrey Quiche** would also be good.

🗨 **Shelleuk**

Wear a hat, carry a cross. Bingo. Hatton Cross.

🗨 **Drew**

Go to www.partysuperstores.co.uk at Clapham Junction (020 7924 3210). They have a list of 30-odd underground stations you can go as.

My favourite was a two person entry – Barbican – where you dress up as Barbie and Ken! Alternately, it's a lot more expensive, but *Angels* (www.fancydress.co.uk) at Cambridge Circus on Shaftesbury Avenue has a similar listing with ideas like Queen Vicoria, Turn-em Green, Black-friars, Shepherds Bush etc.

🗨 **Hun**

Turn up two hours after the party starts, smoking a joint, and you can be Leytonstone(d).

Or just arrive with Kelly Brooke/George Clooney on your arm and you can be Turnham Green.

🗨 **Tim**

I went to a tube party a few years ago with a comedy rubber willy and a can of Australian lager (i.e. Cockfosters. How we laughed.) but undeniably the best costume was on a bloke who was dressed as a massive lobster, wearing a crown and holding a sceptre.

What the fu—? I hear you ask.

The answer: King Crustacean (King's Cross station... oh never mind.)

⌐ **Dr Bone**

Fancy Dress 101 dictates that, boy or girl, you simply don a Fat Face fleece, some purple trousers and a braying voice, et voila! You're a Sloane Square...

⌐ **ils**

Last week there was a beach party on the Thames. It's a semi-regular thing apparently and has been going on for years. I went to a similar one back in April and it was a bit of a let-down, but this week-end's was a fantastic party. Good music, jugglers etc. If you've missed out on Glastonbury this year, keep your eyes peeled at www.swarming.org.uk to find out when you'll next have the chance to get your trainers dirty dancing outside.

It's all dependent on the tides, so you might end up going from 11pm to 5am, although there have been daytime events too. See you there!

⌐ **Anon**

Ah, all this talk of tube parties reminds me of those two weeks a few years back when they were considered fashionable. I arrived at one as the predictable High Barnet (big wig) with a young lady who hadn't realised the party theme. She was wearing her typical leather skirt and biker jacket with big leather boots. The host answered the door with 'don't tell me: High Barnet and King's Cross – back entrance?'. She left in tears.

💬 **ThPhphThphh**

DANCE THE NIGHT AWAY

Does anybody know a good salsa class? I'm trying to teach my boyfriend how to dance with rhythm (rather than a circa 1991 shoulder roll).

💬 **Caroline**

Look, there's no such thing as a good salsa class. Salsa is rubbish. Your boyfriend doesn't want to salsa, trust me. If he says he does, he's lying. He wants to use the early '90s shoulder roll. Let him. If he claps his hands and slowly shuffles backwards, so much the better. When you're at weddings and parties or even at the infernally rubbish 'Down Mexico Way', dancing betwixt greasy faux-Mexican men who are unsubtly trying to get into nice young women's pants, nobody wants to see a couple Salsa-ing with gusto and ability. They'll think you're gits, wannabe Michael Douglas/Catherine Zeta-Jones. Salsa is dead, get over it.

💬 **Matthew**

I'm with Matthew on this. Salsa is a bad thing. I remember when I first moved to London my then girlfriend *insisted* that we attend Salsa classes, for the vague and unassailable reason that it's the sort of thing people do in London of an evening. Young and innocent as I was at the time, I didn't have the wherewithal to shout 'fuck off, no way, you control-freak bitch who is about to run off with my best friend and ruin my life'. Instead I said 'okay'. So we gamely attended the Salsa class on the boat moored near Temple, every bloody week for months.

And it was nonsense. A bunch of wide-eyed and socially-confused girls, a smattering of reluctant boyfriends and a sprinkling of middle-aged male weirdos who were only there for the body contact. All run by a show-off midget with silly hips and bad hair, who made all the men feel stupid and all the women feel like they were Ginger bloody Rogers. I hated him. I still do.

Salsa only exists for 3 reasons:
1) to ruin relationships;
2) to give lonely men erections; and
3) to perpetuate the sad myth that Latin dancing is a heterosexual activity.
It should be banned.

💬 **Charlie**

Salsa at *La Finca* on Pentonville Road between Angel and King's Cross is pretty friendly and neither sad singles nor clingy smugs frequent it. Even as a rubbish British-born prudish bloke I found the classes (beginner/inter/improver/show-off) pretty well structured and a laugh. It gets a bit more scary when the experts do their thing while beginners hang around and practice the one step they learnt in the lesson.

💬 **Dave**

For a non-threatening Salsa Bar, try *Bar Cuba* in Kensington High Street. I haven't been for a couple of years, but they used to run classes early in the evening Monday through Wednesday with a club afterwards.

It always used to be frequented by people who really wanted to dance rather than have a quick grope. I'm a single female and never felt uncomfortable there on these nights. The tapas is very good too. Weekends however maybe a different story, but it's not so much fun then anyway, as it gets very crowded and there's no room to dance properly.

💬 **Voet**

There's a salsa night at the *Buffalo Bar* in Highbury and Islington (Victoria Line). Lesson 7–9pm, then dancing 'til 3am.

Only hitch is it's on a Monday night. I'm a South-Londoner but I still made it a weekly event ('til I became a teacher and school nights out were banned). Do give it a go – you'll really enjoy it. Pretty cheap too, with some fit Cubans (although this isn't a guarantee).

💬 **little miss**

There are two bars in New Cross that have salsa classes – *The Goldsmiths Tavern* and *The Paradise Bar*, both on Monday nights and both on the main road.

💬 **Lolly**

Bar Cuba on Kensington High Street. Sunday 5:30–6:30pm (Beginner/Intermediate); 6:30–7:30pm (Improver/Advanced) Teachers: Orod and Dessi (and team).

I've been to their class here for a couple of years (on and off) and it's very friendly with everyone there to dance. Good atmosphere – no clique-ish behaviour – and everyone is encouraged to dance with everyone (especially someone you've never danced with before).

They have other classes too, dotted around London throughout the week. They also have a website at www.cubandance.com.

🖵 **Piggywigs**

As Caroline's boyfriend (who allegedly dances without rhythm and in a circa 1991 shoulder roll style), I have to admit that I was slightly worse for wear when I agreed to her suggestion but the truth is that I mainly agreed to it for her benefit. She dances with all the style and rhythm of Chris Eubank circa 1991. Don't get me wrong, Chris had a certain elegance in his prime and Caroline does move well. Unfortunately she lacks the ear to limb movement co-ordination and in full flow looks more like a drunken boxer than a stylish mover. Again, it is for this reason that I will join her at these classes.

🖵 **Alleged rhythmless boyfriend**

BELLY

A while back in my more youthful years I worked in a bar in Turkey that did belly dancing. It seemed like a good laugh so I gave it a go. It was great fun and I had a tum to be proud of.

Now, I've been back a few years and have indulged myself with a few too many glasses of wine and far too much good food. I now have a little pot belly which I hate. I know some people think these are cute, but I long for the days of a toned tum. Does anyone know of anywhere that holds belly dancing classes in the West London area? I would love to give it another go, it makes exercise seem like good fun...

🗩 Feebs

In reply to Feebs' enquiry about belly dancing classes, I too was thinking about giving it a go and found a lady who holds classes in Turnham Green on Fridays (*School of Musical Theatre*, Bath Road). £5/hour for all ages and body types /fitness. She also does classes in the Ladbroke Grove area and I believe she also does private one-to-one tuition and home visits. Her name is Kay Spillane, tel. 07941 305 782 or e-mail ms_kaysha@hotmail.com.

Haven't actually plucked up the courage to do it myself yet so don't know if she's any good, but worth contacting all the same.

🗩 Babyangel

Check out *Danceworks* opposite *Selfridges* in London – they have belly dance workshops.

🗩 Lolo

I missed the original post but if you're looking for a class in South East London, can I suggest Elaine? She has classes on a Monday night at the Community Hall, Library, Southwood Road, New Eltham SE9. Email: bellydanceelaine@hotmail.com. Happy wobbling!

💬 **Peggy**

JIVE

Does anyone know where a couple in the middle of love's young dream can find somewhere to learn to jive? Quickly, before it wears off!

💬 **pockettiger**

Give Ceroc a go. It's not strictly jive, more a combination of jive and salsa, but it's got all the swinging and jumping and it's great fun! The music varies from old stuff to the present day and you can go alone or with a partner (dancers are swapped round after each move in the class so you get to dance with everyone). For more information visit: www.ceroc.com or for more specific London info: www.ceroclondon.com.

💬 **Charl**

The Space on the Isle of Dogs does Jive lessons on a Wednesday evening (I think, but am not sure). They have a website but it's not very informative (www.thespace.org.uk), I'd give them a call or check out the free *Wharf* newspaper available in Canary Wharf for listings.

💬 **Leia**

There are loads of places you can learn to jive in London – have a look at: www.uk-jive.co.uk.

There is also a lindy hop class in Balham on Tuesdays at 7.30pm – upstairs at the *Bedford* if you are in that area and feel like something rather more challenging. Maybe not for beginners though, unless you are particularly lithe. For the person who was looking for belly dancing, try: www.cdet.org.uk. They have loads of useful dance information on there – including places where you can do belly dancing.

🖵 **Nancy Drew**

www.learntojive.com does exactly what it says on the tin. I've never been but I've heard them recommended.

🖵 **Katkin**

Things to see

FLICKS

Anybody out there know of a fancy cinema at the 'luxury' end of the market where one can take one's partner or friends to watch a new film? I'm fed up with annoying kids spilling popcorn onto me in the multiplexes. Surely there is an alternative.

🖵 **Xpablo**

If you're looking for a luxury cinema, then look no further than *The Electric* in Portobello Road.

www.electriccinema.co.uk. Big red leather armchairs with matching footstools, and a small table with built-in wine cooler between each chair. Very useful as there's a bar at the back of the hall. Utter genius – you'll never go to a multiplex again.

The Electric can be booked for private functions, along with (I believe) the exclusive members-only bar. Alternatively, *One Aldwych* (www.onealdwych.co.uk) has a screening room which be can hired out and will even show your home movies if you like.

Normally open only to hotel residents, mere mortals can get in on a special deal where you get dinner and a glass of champagne included for £35. Sounds ace but I've not been there myself (except for dinner at *Indigo*, which was ace indeed).

💬 **Stocky**

The *National Film Theatre* has a deal where if you guarantee to bring a certain number of people you can book a fave film for a special occasion. These do then get advertised to other people, so you'll have a few blow-ins, especially if it is a popular film, but I must say that they seem like a nice lot that go there. This is for film only, no food or drinks, but plenty of nice places nearby for before or after, especially al fresco in the summer.

www.bfi.org.uk/showing/nft/index.html.

Note: as there is no food or drink allowed, this is a fantastic place to see films without being annoyed. Also nearly everyone who goes there is really keen on films and an attentive audience. Even given to rounds of applause on rare occasions, which I love. And you get a nice leaflet reviewing the film, even for blockbuster current releases.

💬 **Zed**

The *UCI* in Greenwich has an area called *The Gallery*. It's £15 each, but you do get super-wide leather seats (in pairs and the arms come up so you can get rather comfy with your partner), free popcorn, sweets, nachos, soft drinks and coffees. There's even a licensed bar with proper glass glasses which you can take into the cinema with you. And the staff will even serve you more coffee mid-show without you leaving your seat. £15 well spent in my opinion.

Rich Rich

The *Odeon* cinema in Golders Green was always empty on Friday nights due to the fact that the local Jewish community have faith-based commitments. Alas, it has since closed down and I no longer live in the area but there must be a cinema in or near Golders Green, and on Fridays it should be very quiet indeed.

Atheist

The Prince Charles Cinema in Leicester Square hires out its auditorium for private parties. www.princecharlescinema.com.

Anon

A very cool little cinema that maybe worth renting out a screen from is *Screen* on Baker Street – and they have a bar too. Otherwise you could try the screening rooms that the industry use in Soho – I think one is called *Mr Young's* but I may be totally off the mark.

Mistress

Some time ago someone highlighted the amazingly lovely screening room at the *Aldwych* hotel on the Strand. I just wanted to say thank you. They have a special thing on called Give Me Dinner and Movies, where you get an amazing three-course meal, with lots of choice on the menu, a glass of champers and a film in their blue Italian leather, 30-seat screening room. I was looking for something cool to celebrate my 35th – and this was fab!

Cocktails, champers, dinner, the coolest disco-style lift (check it out and you'll know what I mean) I've ever seen and Steven McQueen in *The Thomas Crown Affair*. What more could a (old) girl ask for?

💬 **SparkleT**

DRAG

I have to organise my sister's hen night and I want to take us all to a cabaret/drag-show-type thingy. *Madame Jo-Jo's* has been suggested but I wanted somewhere a little more off the beaten track. It just needs to be relatively central, with decent food and good entertainment – does anyone have any ideas?? I'm at my wit's end!

💬 **Emma**

There is a club at the *Vauxhall Tavern* in Vauxhall called *Duckies*. I think it's a weekly event. I experienced the show at the *Barbican* where they were doing a Christmas residency involving the performers coming to your table and doing a private performance for a Duckie dollar, a very good night to get drunk, loud and leery.

💬 **Kite**

The *Black Cap* in Camden has an excellent drag/cabaret show. Haven't got round to going myself as yet, but it might be worth a look! www.theblackcap.com.

💬 **Cinders**

And finally...

PIPE UP

Does anyone know where you can practise the bagpipes in London? My flatmate needs somewhere (anywhere, just *not* the flat). We're in Clapham but I'm not sure it would go down too well on the Common on a sunny Sunday afternoon. Can you hire sound-proof music rooms for that kind of thing? What a shame this isn't Edinburgh and he could just go and busk in the street!

Scottie Scottie

Scottie Scottie, I don't know you but by your description of your flatmate I have a feeling his name is Craig?

He's already been spotted by someone I know atop a mound of earth on Clapham Common, piping his lungs out for whoever will listen. I suggest you hire one of those Big Yellow Self Storage spaces and let him practice in there.

Granty

There is a nice little rehearsal studio under the arches at Clapham Junction that I used to use with my band. Its quite basic but cosy and you can make as much noise as you like. We used to get it for 35 quid for 4 hours on a Saturday. www.breakfaststudios.co.uk.

Clefty

Did this bagpipe player live on Lavender Hill a couple of years ago? As I remember when I lived there, looking out my living room window to the flat opposite (above and to the right of *The Beaufoy* pub) a guy used to practice bagpipes stood in the window, occasionally wearing nothing but a kilt with a strobe light behind him so he was impossible to miss from the street below/flat opposite. I would have liked to ask him to keep the noise down but as you can imagine, he looked a bit psychotic.

The Horse

Transport

Ask any Londoner what the single most irritating thing about the capital is, and you can guarantee they'll say the same thing: Burberry baseball caps. But press them for a slightly less obvious irritation and they'll probably mumble something about transport. And who can blame them? The tube continues to go off the rails, the overland trains are crowded and late and even good old Routemaster looks destined for scrap. But despite all that, LBLers are still surprisingly fond of our rickety old transport network. In this section we consider some of the peculiar moments that make tube travel almost bearable, we uncover London's secret tunnel network, we get into a tussle about bus doors and wonder why there are so few water taxis.

All aboard!

People moving

FELLOW TRAVELLERS

Picture the scene – its late Thursday night, an underground carriage full of people slowly winds its way south, picking up the last of the office workers and pub goers, taking them back home after a long day and longer night. Everything appears to be normal, nothing out of the ordinary – the same places, the same blank faces. That is until a group returning home from a Lemon Jelly gig decide to blow up a balloon and start passing it about – first to each other, then to others, until gradually a whole section of the carriage is in on the bizarre act of balloon keepy-uppy. People got on and people got off and still the game continued, with each stop bringing new players – and for the first time I can remember people actually talked to each other and smiled at each other and waved and said goodbye when they departed for their beds.

I realise this all sounds a bit surreal and I think it was really, but after 27 years living in London its nice to know that the people sat around you on the tube aren't all that bad after all, and that people can be friendly, and be silly enough not to take everything too seriously. With things the way they are in London and the world at the moment, seeing people smile and mess about has changed my outlook a little (even if a little alcohol had been consumed by all!) and gives me some hope that things could get better, if even hardened Londoners can occasionally let their guards down!

We made it from Kentish Town as far as Balham before the balloon burst, but its replacement made it all the way to Morden – good skills shown by everyone involved, especially the lady who got off at Balham whose hair made balloon one burst.

Same time next week?

Bryan

I was on one of the last Northern line trains back from the West End on a Saturday night, having spent most of the evening being reminded why I never go out there anymore (stag dos, hen nights, millions of tourists, lots of 16 year olds) when the most hilarious camp bloke got on and started reciting *Les Miserables* at top volume.

He did have the programme so the words were at least right. He was awful but getting away with it in the way that only outrageous gay men can. Anyway, a girl opposite me was laughing and we caught each other's eye and proceeded to glance at each other and smile about every five minutes for the rest of the journey.

Now I know that this would normally border on the weird for average tube journeys, but I feel compelled to say that it utterly made my night. You forget how nice it is for someone just to smile at you occasionally. Helps if it's an attractive girl, obviously. Maybe it was just good because it never happens, but maybe everyone would be happier if it happened all the time. I might risk being a freak for a couple of weeks and see what happens...

Greg

I was on my way to work at 7am one morning, just to beat the heat wave when it is unbearable to be in the tube. We got to Golders Green and this guy came on the train. Looked around, a little bit apprehensive and then opened his bag and brought out a bowl and started munching away.

Within minutes the whole carriage was filled with the smell of curry and he did not give a toss. Finished his meal, put his plate away, slouched on the dirty seats and started snoring. I looked at him with a smile on my face and, being a country bumpkin, would like to say, London, I salute you.

🗨 Fadders

HOOK

Have any of you seen the man who seems to have found the perfect way of keeping his suit jacket in good shape while travelling the tubes? I've seen this guy a couple of different times, on both the Central and the District line. Basically he sits next to the doors where the little glass partition is and whips one of those hooks with a little sucker on the back, plonks it up on the glass, hangs his jacket up and then sits and reads his paper like its the most normal thing to do in the world.

Maybe there's an unexploited market for sucker hooks, not just for your bathroom door.

🗨 El Capitan

I haven't seen the bloke with the hook for his jacket, but has anyone seen a bloke on the High Barnet branch of the Northern line who loops his jacket over one of the overhead bars as a prelude to muttering incomprehensibly while gathering up all of the old newspapers in the carriage and tearing out the articles which appear to offend his sensibilities? Unsurprisingly *Metro* seems to require a lot of tearing.

🗨 Naeonlite

Don't you just hate it when those bus drivers don't wait when you're trying to buy a ticket from those machines? I blame that Ken Livingstone.

🗩 Miss Moneypenny

In response to Miss Moneypenny's aside about bus drivers not waiting while people buy tickets from the machines, the whole point of the machines is to speed up boarding so the bus can get people to their destination faster! If the bus driver waits for latecomers to get their tickets it's pretty pointless.

🗩 Crouch Ender

COUGH

As if bus/train/tube journeys aren't already miserable enough, we all know when the cold and flu season is upon us by the fact that every carriage/bus/platform sounds like an infirmary. As I sat on the tube today and a man plopped down next to me and proceeded to splutter, gasp, gulp and hack non-stop throughout the journey, I wondered to myself – what is it with these people?

They seem to think that shrugging their shoulders and making a crinkly face when a big sneeze comes on is somehow acceptable simply because they can't be bothered to raise one of their hands to cover their mouth and nose.

I can't imagine that any of those disgusting and vile monsters number amongst the LBL readership. But just in case any of us is attacked by a ghastly virus, can I suggest that we prepare some ground rules? Here's my list for starters.

a) Behave yourself. Stop pretending like you don't remember what your mum taught you about manners when you're ill.

b) Do not breathe on anyone else. Do not go near anyone else. Stay home. Or if you insist on travelling by public transport when you're so sick, take measures to ensure that your breath/snot/spit does not stray into anyone else's personal space. Just because some other careless idiot gave you a virus doesn't mean you should take it out on the next guy.

c) Take some cold medicine for God's sake. That's why it exists.

d) Carry some Kleenex in your pocket. Don't think you don't need it. You can't possibly believe that we don't notice you surreptitiously wiping your wet, sneezed-in, germ-covered hand on your trousers and then on the handrail.

I thank you, and we all thank you, for your co-operation.

💬 Sergeant Matron

In regard to Sergeant Matron's worthy slating of the sick-but-inconsiderate and Annie's sick-on-the-tube horror story one name comes to mind: Robert Bloody Elms. He's the type of (north) Londonite that would just smile in a crinkly way and go 'Naar: being sick and sneezing on people in London's just brilliant, it makes London the cosmopolitan, scruffy, marvellous, topsy-turvy old place we all love... just like in *Withnail and I*!'.

I don't see it like that. I think people treat the tube like crap and should wake up. For starters don't eat or drink! If you don't smoke on the tube, don't do this! Seeing people casually stow their empty cans and sandwich holders behind them á la *Metro* makes me sick.

That would help for starters.

💬 Damien

HONK

After ten years in the capital, I thought I'd seen it all when it comes to the grottiness levels of Londoners. However, I saw something on the Victoria line last week that shocked even me and I'd be interested to know if I imagined it or if another subscriber was in the same carriage and can act as a corroborating witness.

Around mid-afternoon, I was standing in the middle of a tube carriage pulling in to King's Cross station. Three people stood up to get out and proceeded to walk towards the door to my left. One of them made a very guttural sound and then sprayed what looked like a good few litres of clear liquid over the back of the man in front of him, on to the legs and handbags of two pensioners to his right and the trousers of two businessmen to his left.

He then got out, the doors to the tube shut and one of the businessmen turned to the other and asked him what had just happened. 'That bloke was just sick all over us,' came the reply. Did anyone change seats? Did they spontaneously vomit themselves at the gastric horror of it all? Not a bit of it. The pensioners quietly wiped their handbags down with handkerchiefs, the businessmen wiggled the legs of their trousers and we all watched the remaining puke roll around the floor.

Now I know we Brits are famous for our stiff upper lips but it has to be some kind of mutant British reserve that adapts to being copiously honked on in the middle of the afternoon by a total stranger and produces only a ruffled hanky in response. Or maybe I'm just some hysterically uptight, anal freak.

🗨 Annie

Annie's tale of a vomiting tube passenger is not exceptional. About two years ago (on my second day at a new job), I was stood on a particularly crowded Vicky line tube pulling into Oxford Circus. As we pulled in, I heard (over the noise of my personal stereo) an alien sound, and felt something hit the back of my leg.

Unable to turn round due to reasons of space, I waited a few seconds till the door opened before turning to discover vomit all over the back of my jeans. As I bellowed 'FUCKING HELL!' at the top of my considerable lungs, I witnessed the vomiter running through the crowds making good her escape.

Lucky for her; I'd have murdered her.

Still, it broke the ice with my new colleagues. 'Sorry, can I have 15 minutes off to buy some new trousers? Some little tyke vommed on mine this morning'.

💬 Dr Bone

POET

Has anyone else seen the busker/tube poet who tells the awful rhyme about the tube? I saw him last week on the Northern line at about 6pm (not my normal line thank God). He is quite skinny, with a skinhead, except for a strange long strand of blue hair protruding from the front.

He gets on the train and says something like 'Ladies and Gentleman, can I have a moment of your time?'. (Which is tantamount to saying 'I am a tramp or a nutter and about to hideously embarrass you.') He then recites a 'poem' about tube commuting which I wish for the life of me I could remember, but it's something like:

- **A is for the arseholes that we travel with everyday,**
- **B is for Bureaucracy that always makes you pay,**

And so on. Actually I made the above two up, but some actual ones were:

- J is for the Jealousy for those that have a seat,
- M is for the announcer saying 'Mind the Gap',
- N is for the Newspaper that's always full of crap,
- P is for the Pervert who is staring at your crotch...

He went through the whole alphabet, during which there were a few smiles from the passengers and then lots of shuffling, as it was going on a bit too long and we wondered what he'd do at the end. When he did actually finish, there was a silence, and he said 'Ah come on folks – you can do better than that'. Still nothing. Then he looked all hurt and stood in the corner swigging from a bottle of mineral water and got off at the next stop.

Does the poor man do this every day? Does anyone else know the whole poem or can you fill in some of the lines?

💬 Annie Mole

This morning, by Chancery Lane tube, I saw a man casually tossing an empty chocolate milk carton out of his van window onto the pavement. I was outraged – waving my fist, fetching up the offending carton in my righteous grasp, and shrieking at the top of my lungs, I castigated him for his ignorance and incivility. All right – I didn't. I scowled quietly. But I want to know: if you see someone throwing litter in the street, are you allowed to tell them to pick it up or does that just make you a wanker?

💬 Sue P

I too have seen the dreadful tube poet – also on the Northern line a couple of months ago. He introduced himself by saying that he wasn't a beggar but a 'professional street entertainer' – which is an acceptable definition when you're are entertaining on a street and your potential audience has a choice about whether to stop or walk straight past, but if you're reduced to relying on captive audiences trapped in tube trains I feel that according yourself professional status may be wishful thinking.

Anyway, not only did he read his dreadful poem, but he then compounded his crimes by doing some juggling from an unexplained crouching position.

As far as I remember, some people clapped.

🗨 Curmudgeon

Underground

SECRETS

Near Gloucester Road underground station, if you walk along the tube tracks for two minutes (toward South Kensington on the District line) and turn left down a small passage before you actually reach South Kensington, there is the remains of a small shop which looks like an old fashioned newsagents. The windows are broken, and it's very tatty; but the question I have to ask is, what is it doing there all that way underground?

🗨 James

Hmm... well the random sweetie shop in the middle of the tube could be for sweet-toothed refugees. There are billions of weird unused and secret tunnels around London. There are tons of abandoned bits of the Northern line with spaces big enough for people to live in, and they did.

In Clapham, by Clapham South tube and also by the big Sainsbury's car park, there are these big, round, not very high concrete towers which were once used as homes and have access to loads of other tunnels. I think they were actually used as temporary accommodation for Caribbeans that came over in the '50s.

After the people's applications to live here had been processed and they had been given passports, etc they were then allowed out of the tubes to go and live wherever they liked. As Brixton was nearby and cheap, many of them went there and invited friends and family to join them. I think that's it.

💬 Polly

Has anyone else seen the lady on the tube (seen at Westminster station changing between the Jubilee and District and Circle lines) who travels with her cat draped on her shoulders, or was I hallucinating? The lady was glaring at people, but the cat seemed perfectly at ease...

And does one have to purchase a ticket to take a creature on the tube, and what counts – children, yes. Dogs? Cats? Small reptiles?

💬 Pockettiger

I was just wondering what James was doing wandering 'two minutes along the tracks towards South Kensington'. I mean, well done for finding a ex-newsagents in a tunnel but presumably he, or someone like him, is the reason my journey was delayed by something like 30 minutes the other day while the power had to be switched off and the police went to retrieve people who were half-way down a tunnel.

If I've got the wrong end of the stick, apologies. If, however, you are the sort of person that goes wandering along train tracks unnecessarily, please could you ensure you do it a) when I am not on a train trying to get across London and b) in black clothes, so that the chances of removing your genes from the pool are higher.

💬 Jonny

I was intrigued by the hidden subterranean newsagent at Gloucester Road tube. Recently I was listening to the Robert Elms show on BBC London (or whatever they call it now) and it was being discussed as part of a discussion about hidden underground buildings. Someone phoned in and explained what it was about. Apparently there used to be a record shop, newsagent and ticket offices at the station. This was in the early '70s. A few years later – mid-70s the caller thought – the station was redeveloped and a new entrance was built at street level, on top of the old stuff. Perhaps there are still racks of rare old '70s LPs, still on sale at 37/6d, and a wizened old hippie, stash long gone, waiting for the new Jethro Tull LP.

💬 Michael

When I was much younger I used to love the frisson of walking along the tube lines when too drunk to sleep (room-spin, head in bin). The power goes off after 1am and apart from the occasional fox, this 70-foot-wide strip of London is all mine and no-one else's. Sitting on top of a signal gantry watching the summer sun rise over the houses below me was memorable (as was the hangover).

💬 Pretzel

A friend of mine loves the sound of his own voice. No, really loves the sound of his own voice. I mean, it's nice enough, but you know, get over it. A few years back, when he could be quite legitimately called a functioning alcoholic, he would travel to work every day on the tube reading aloud from Winnie the Pooh. He argues it kept him sane, while refusing to accept he probably drove everyone else mad. He was quite offended when I suggested that this made him the tube weirdo, saying that in nine months of oratory, only one person complained. Knowing this as I do, I still wouldn't confront anyone who was annoying the hell of me on the tube. He's now a barrister, by the way.

💬 Nick

Once, when at Westminster tube station, a friend of mine wandered off down a side tunnel on a whim and found a door. Expecting it to be locked, he was surprised to find that it opened to reveal a rather posh-looking room, with wood-panelled walls, another bigger door and a concierge-type person behind a reception desk.

Needless to say he got a strange look and got out of there sharpish. Upon revisiting the door at a later date, he found it locked. What's that all about then? Private tube station for MPs? Or is it a member's club for tube drivers, where they can sip expensive brandy between shifts?

Batfink

There is a round vent on a small raised lawn over the road from the entrance to Westminster Abbey (in front of the Methodist Central Hall). I've heard this is for the miles of 'secret tunnels' under parliament. Is this true? It is not far from the route of the District line so could be a tube vent but it's bugging me.

Plugus Maximus

I worked at *Harrods* for all of about two weeks when I was seventeen. Staff have to enter the building via a door on the other side of the road from *Harrods*, go down some stairs and along a maze of tunnels (underneath the road) to finally come up from the basement of *Harrods* itself.

According to the staff info pack, *Harrods* is also completely self sufficient – it has its own power generator, its own water supply, etc. So if London ever went to war again or for some reason all utilities were stopped, the store could keep functioning as normal.

I'm not sure why or when this was built as it is, but next

time you walk down Knightsbridge, think of all the *Harrods* staff to-ing and fro-ing underneath the pavement beneath you.

 Charl

The huge complex of tunnels under Whitehall does exist. If you visit *The Cabinet War Rooms* you are in a small part of a massive underground office network centred beneath the Treasury. This complex reputedly has over 200 rooms, many of which are still used by the government today. It's quite likely that there is an entrance to the complex in Westminster station for civil servants based in those offices. When Batfink's friend wandered off down that side tunnel on a whim he may well have found the door. That would also explain the rather posh wood-panelled room and the concierge behind a reception desk.

Leading away from the central office complex are a series of tunnels that provide access to other Government buildings in Westminster. One runs north, connecting to the government underground telephone exchange and main telephone network. It has a number of branches and it's rumoured that one of these leads directly from Buckingham Palace to enable the Royal Family to escape to Charing Cross and safety in the country.

Connected to this network is the Post Office bomb-proof telephone trunk system. Stemming from a headquarters near Waterloo Station are two tunnels. One leads to Trafalgar

Is it just me (and I do hope not) or do all the free – oops, I mean bendy – buses smell of, well, poo?

 pockettiger

Square and the Government tunnel complex, the other to
Faraday House in the City. Another tunnel runs from
Shepherds Bush to Shoreditch connecting telephone
exchanges from west to east.

 This system was built during the cold war and consists
of a 16-foot diameter tunnel that also connects with the
Kingsway telephone exchange that was built 100 feet under
High Holborn in the early 1950s.

For more information on what's under High Holborn and
other abandoned tube stations and lines take a look at
www.starfury.demon.co.uk/uground.

💬 Auawsha

SPY

**Having recently returned to the north after seven
years in London, I am slightly gutted that I cannot
easily check out the long abandoned Strand tube
station entrance as featured in the BBC3 documentary, _Spy_.
Could someone please go there, see if the photo booth really
does exist and whether the main door goes anywhere?**

💬 Gil

Yes, the main door does lead to the former ticket area, and
the photo booth is always there. There's quite a good history
of the station here:

 www.starfury.demon.co.uk/uground/aldwych.html.

You can even hire out Aldwych tube (minus the platforms)
for parties – £500 for the night when I did it several years
ago, which is pretty good considering its location. It was,
however, rather difficult keeping a load of inebriated students

away from the old tube signs, which were kept in an
unlocked room out the back.

 Patrick

The photo booth at the old Strand station is really there,
or at least was there several years ago. Boyfriend of the
time and I were walking past and popped in to see if the
booth works. It doesn't but we had a camera so we took our
own photo in the booth anyway. Not sure about the big door.

Ruby ru

There's a guy on the Victoria line who gets on at
Victoria and sits in the carriage cutting his toenails
until he gets off at Stockwell. Luckily for me he only
ever does this once a week but he always seems to
end up in the same carriage.

Solace

The 'long abandoned' Strand tube station? Aldwych, on the Strand, first opened its doors in 1907 and closed only ten years ago. I've been down there since, during London Open House weekend. The lifts don't work (the station closed because it wasn't economic to replace them) but the tannoy does, and you can still get down to the platforms. The station is used for filming, and for testing platform surfaces etc. And yes, there is a photo booth at the entrance.

💬 **Rich**

I didn't see the BBC3 thing, but I do know that the tube station and photo booth are there. The door to the north (on the Strand, near the photo booth) leads into the old lobby, and to the east there is a larger entrance without the long approach.

The lobby of the station is still intact, and much of the underground part of the station is still there. Including the tracks. I believe London Underground occasionally use it to test decorative schemes (although that may be somewhere else, I forget). The lifts don't work any more, my understanding is that they were locked off with RSJs years ago. The station was last in use in about 1986 (but don't quote me on this) when it was better known as 'Aldwych' and was a special branch of the Piccadilly line from Holborn.

The platforms at Holborn are still there, but boarded off. The line was closed when they realised no-one really used it.

I know much of this because a very nice former girlfriend took me to the London Underground summer party held inside the station. This sparked a bit of an interest, so I looked all this nonsense up on the old internetty.

💬 **mudge (tube geek)**

TECHNOLOGY

**Last week I was travelling on the Metropolitan line
eastbound when I noticed a strange tube train
parked at the end of the westbound platform
of Euston Square.**

**It was only three cars long and a quick glance through
the windows as I passed showed it to be stripped of seats
etc., and filled with all kinds of high-tech computery type
things.**

Does anyone know what this train was?

🗭 Tom

The other week I was chatting to somebody in the pub who
tests planes and tube trains to find out the stresses and
pressures put upon passengers and staff. To do this they
control and monitor the temperature, air pressure etc., in
different parts of the train. Maybe this was the mysterious
train that was seen?

🗭 Fineart

**'Even if I had a friend in Clapham, I wouldn't pay a
bloody fiver to visit him.' The best thing about the
congestion charge is that it has massively increased
the North–South divide.**
Discuss.

🗭 LBL

Clapham isn't in the congestion zone.

🗭 C (Clapham)

CHOCOLATE

If you go up to one of the chocolate machines in any tube station and keep pressing a combination of 1s and 0s, a special message appears on the LCD display – a message that all Londoners might do well to heed. I can't tell you what it is or it will spoil the surprise. If anyone can tell me why this message appears I will buy them a bar of chocolate.

Goldenanorak

The magic code for the tube platform chocolate machines that Goldenanorak asked about is 110. When I was at school (how old does that make the machines? A decade? God!), a friend of mine had been out with his girlfriend and bought her some chocolate from one of those machines on the way home. Thing is though, it dished out two bars instead of one. He asked her 'well how do you say thanks to a computer?' She said 'I dunno, but it must involve 1s and 0s. Try 110.'

He did and the little screen responded: 'OK! No problems!' You could have knocked them both down with a feather. I think its actually some sort of system check code used by the engineers to see if there's anything wrong with them, but it still makes me smile to thank the vending machine when I've bought something.

Andrew

The 110 chocolate machine hack is all about getting the message 'OK! No problems!' to come up and not about getting free chocolate. I find whenever I am a bit pissed off on the tube, just seeing that message helps. A bit.

Ian

FALLING DOWN

I was in Oxford Street recently and would just like to mention the poor girls who collapsed because of the heat, one at Oxford Street, and the other at Bond Street.

There were paramedics there within minutes, but surely the time has come for air conditioning on the tube. It is ridiculous the amount of suffering us commuters have to put up with just trying to get around.

Being a former fainter myself (on the tube last year – thank you once again to the kind staff at Harrow on the Hill) I totally sympathise with those girls. It's too hot, it's too crowded, there is no ventilation and no water vending machines! I think LBLers should start a petition as we did with the late night tube. What do you think? Any takers?

🗩 Feebs

Feebs, I'm no engineer, but I think one of the reasons there's no air conditioning on the tube (cost aside) is that there's nowhere to dissipate the heat taken from the chilled air in the trains, except through the stations.

They would then become even more uncomfortably hot than they are now. It might be feasible to have air conditioning on the cut-and-cover lines (District, Circle, Metropolitan, East London) because they have a lot more ways for the hot air to escape to the outside world, but on the deep-level lines I fear it's not going to happen.

Water dispensers, on the other hand, seem like a great idea. Just spare a thought for the poor mite that has to pick up everyone's discarded cups.

🗩 General Joy

Air conditioning on the tube seems pretty unlikely, given the huge cost, but why can't there be a vending machine for bottles of water on each platform instead of those rubbish chocolate machines?

There are a few water vending machines around the tube network but there's a couple of chocolate machines on every platform. London Underground's own advice is to carry water during hot weather so why don't they help us out?

Surely there would be plenty of companies happy to install vending machines on the platforms (as long as they don't really rip you off)? London Underground could even introduce its own branded water...

⌐⌐ **Crouch Ender**

I agree that our recent scorching hot summers have made the tube unbearable at best and dangerous at worst. However, the fact is that our tube system, apart from being the oldest in the world, is too deep and too narrow to install air conditioning units.

For air conditioning to function, you need the space to push hot air out which we clearly do not have in the LU tunnels. Also, on most lines, the tube is nowhere near the surface, making it impossible to extract hot air generated by the AC units. Think of New York – the subway is literally a few feet under the pavement, and the Paris Metro – the tunnels are spacious and wide – both providing conditions where AC units can be installed.

Alas, when our tube system was built, the AC unit was but a twinkle in its Daddy's eye. Add to that, far more numbers using the tube than it was ever designed to accommodate. I have heard of an AC unit that doesn't require the environment I've just described to work but they would cost literally millions of pounds to acquire and install.

I guess LU's feeling on this matter is that this hot weather only occurs a few weeks every year and, what with the crumbling tube system as it is, they cannot justify this amount of money being spent. I'd advise you to petition on improving the system generally so that it doesn't have so many hold-ups and bottlenecks so as to at least keep you, and the air, moving!

🖵 **Tubeworm**

Cadbury's have the rights to all food/drink vending machines on London Underground, so if you're thinking of setting up a water company to rival them, you'll be playing with the big boys.

I have it on very good authority though that they are replacing a whole bunch of those totally pointless and frequently jammed choccy machines with drinks vending machines that will be supplying Malvern water to all you thirsty tube-goers (not me though, I'll take the bus any day over that sweaty death-trap).

Can't help you on the price though I'm afraid. No doubt they will try and fleece all the pennies they can get.

🖵 **strangeciara**

The soft drinks vending contract for the tube is with Coca-Cola until 2007. Pepsi had the contract until 1997, but couldn't come up with a good enough design for a vending machine. They have to be slim and high capacity. Coke were trialling them in 2002. That's all I know.

🖵 **Ray**

I emailed London Underground to ask why they didn't have more water vending machines on platforms instead of those rubbish chocolate machines – especially as they advise passengers to carry water in hot weather (should we ever get any!).

This was their response:

'The vending machines are not run by London Underground but by private companies who are leasing the platform space for their own products. London Underground currently does not want to divert much-needed funds into a commercial project for selling non-transport oriented products to its customers.'

It seems very shortsighted to me as they could presumably make money from this – and also avoid delays when passengers pull the emergency alarm because they feel faint on the train.

💬 Crouch Ender

SEEING STARS

I've wondered this for years – what are the blue, five-pointed star-shaped stickers that you sometimes see in tube carriages (usually on the ceiling), particularly on the Circle line?

When I was younger I thought they were coded messages from/for the IRA – 'train marked for bombing' or something like that. I feel fairly sure now that this isn't the case.

💬 **Tim**

I am a tube driver on a busy line. Sorry to disappoint you but they are not there to alert the IRA or anything sinister like that. They are simply to remind drivers of the location of vital equipment on the train should we require access to them in an emergency.

💬 **Tube Guru**

'I am a tube driver on a busy line' was enough to prompt me to ask 'what's it like?' In a sad way a bit similar to that video of travel around the M25, I'd love to sit up front and see what the view's like.

Can I? Go on. Can you at least get a video?

💬 **Damian**

Damian – if you want to see what sort of view a tube driver enjoys, try sitting at the front of a DLR train as it departs from Bank station. It will travel through a short, dark tunnel, presumably not dissimilar from those found on the underground.

💬 **Al**

As with any job, driving a tube train does have its positive and negative points. It does get very boring at times but I have had other jobs and I wouldn't swap it for the world. Besides, have you not read in *Metro* how wonderful our benefits are? As for coming up front with me... hmm, I can see the potential for moonlighting and earning a bit of extra cash selling tube rides.

💬 Tube Guru

CRACKING THE CODE

Can anyone tell me what the coded message that I sometimes hear over the public address system in tube stations means? The message is 'Can Inspector Sands please report to room something-or-other', and is usually repeated four or five times, to the general scurryment of surrounding staff. I've heard it in three stations now and it's quite obviously a recorded message and the most blatant code for something I've ever been witness to. But nothing obvious ever seems to be happening, so what is it?

💬 Jacquelyn

Any calls for 'Inspector Sands' are code for the fact that a fire alarm has been activated somewhere in the system and that the staff should see if there's really a fire around or if the alarm has been set off by dust or someone messing about.

It's said in this way so that people don't panic like crazy and stampede out of the station. It refers to the sand that used to be in old fire buckets.

A friend of mine made a recording of the announcement at Aldgate that you can hear here:

www.foxtravel.fsbusiness.co.uk/tube/sands1.mp3.

💬 Annie

Those Inspector Sands announcements on the tubes are a coded security message, asking staff to check out a suspicious package or whatever as a prelude to possibly clearing the station.

At the government's biannual arms bazaar, on the press day when it wasn't only the arms dealers and their clients there, the equivalent message if they wanted the arms salespeople to search their stalls during a security alert was to say over the PA that 'a rare prayer book had been lost'.

Usually in such situations, like with the Inspector Sands one, you can tell that the seemingly one-off announcement is fishy since it's so obviously pre-recorded.

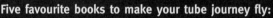 Albert

Five favourite books to make your tube journey fly:
1. *The Sexual Life of Catherine M* by Catherine Miller recommended by KT.
2. *The Art of Living* by the Dalai Lama recommended by BeeG.
3. *London* by Edward Rutherford recommended by Monkavich.
4. *On the Road* by Jack Kerouac recommended by Sudonim.
5. *London: The Biography* by Peter Ackroyd recommended by Meanhim.

LBL

DOORS

Does anyone know why tubes are fitted with 'open' buttons on the doors? These obviously have no effect on the actual opening of the door as this power has been granted solely to the driver.

Something that drives me mad is when people continuously press the button (as if running the 100m on *Daley Thompson's Decathalon*) in vain to gain entry. Something that winds me up even more is when they accidentally time the pressing of the button with the driver opening the doors anyway – they misguidedly think they did it.

You didn't just do that, OK? Stop thinking it was down to you. This isn't a Thames Turbo you know. All the doors open at the same time.

 Scally

All this talk of not being able to open tube doors yourself reminds me of something that happened to my girlfriend. She's Irish and despite having lived in London for a year got stuck on a BR train. When I say stuck, I mean she just wasn't able to get off, as the doors didn't open. Mind you, she didn't actually push the button by the door as apparently the tube doors always opened for her. Don't get caught out in the same way...

 Mark

Overground

BUSSEDING OUT

Sometimes, you are on a bus and you are running late and the bus isn't moving, but the driver won't let you off the bus even though it is only a pathetic 20 yards to the stop. Very annoying. The other day that exact thing happened to me on London Bridge and I have discovered a cunning plan to get off the bus. Only to use when you are really, truly late and it is safe to do. Above the main doors there is a black hood-shaped thing which is the emergency door opener I think. There is a lever in there and if you twist it, hey presto! The doors open.

No doubt the driver will shout at you but he won't be able to do much if you scarper pretty speedily. Plus the other delayed travellers will be very pleased with you.

⌨ **Polly**

Polly's idea of using the emergency door release to get out of a bus is very innovative but unfortunately it could prove very expensive.

I believe that you can be fined for improper use of the release handle and most bus doorways are fitted with CCTV nowadays so even if you scarper you will probably be caught on camera!

⌨ **Martinez**

To the person who has just discovered the emergency door release handle on buses: well done – but what took you so long?

I am a slightly shorter-than-average person who can't reach said button and has to sit in abject despair of a morning. So keep it up. You are a true hero.

💬 **Mike**

Polly, I'd suggest getting up earlier. We all know that a lot of bus drivers tend to be a bit psychotic in London but I don't know how I'd cope with a heap of pompous, self-aware, egocentric and self-righteous so-and-sos letting off steam at my expense, not to mention risking their own safety by doing something that no doubt shouldn't be done and would possibly compromise your safety and the driver's job. Remain seated.

💬 **Damian**

ALARMED

I just saw an empty bus outside Finsbury Park station, with a loud siren going off, alternating with an equally loud recorded message: 'This bus is under attack! Please dial 999! Waaah! Waaah!' The message was being read out in a silly, squeaky voice. The driver was standing by his bus, looking unconcerned.

Have any other readers come across buses that were under attack? Been on board at the time? Or perhaps attacked the odd bus themselves?

💬 **ATP**

I've been on a bus that was under attack – a gang were kicking out the windows on the upper deck of a number 73 – and not only was the bus alarm set off (the same person with the ridiculous voice was whining for help) but the conductor's ticket machine also had a separate alarm. While the driver was completely chilled out, the conductor was terrified and it was all a bit horrible. I don't know about you lot, but when I was 15 I spent my time constructively drinking Merrydown gold top in the park, not kicking out bus windows and generally being really intimidating.

🗨 **Bus Guru**

I've been on a bus under attack – I was on a number 25 from Aldgate to Ilford and this guy got on at Stratford and started arguing with the driver because he couldn't change his £20 note.

The bus was packed, and other people at the front were offering to pay his fare for him, as he had no change but he kept refusing and arguing with the driver, and then refused to get off.

This went on until we got to Forest Gate, when the passenger started hitting the plastic screen protecting the driver. The driver pulled the bus over and activated the alarm (yes, that same whiny voice you referred to) and opened the doors, as this bloke kept on hitting the screen. He eventually managed to hit it so hard that it cracked and flew out of its frame and onto the pavement through the open door.

People started getting off and I was the only person who called the police, while of course pretty much all the other passengers were perfectly content to stand on the pavement watching this poor bus driver getting his face smacked in. The guy ran off while I was still on the phone to the police, and not one person tried to stop him.

I ended up making a statement at Stratford police station but I don't know if anything ever came of it. It was scary, and it was the first and only time in all of my 32 years that I've ever had to dial 999 but I'd do it again if it meant saving someone from a smacking (and if you're wondering why I didn't actually wade in myself, I'm a girly and didn't fancy my chances. I don't know what excuse the very well-built guy watching from the pavement would give, though).

💬 PeeGee

THINK, BIKE

I know that cycling is the most efficient way of getting anywhere in London. It's quick (halved the length of my journey to work) and cheap (saves me £40 a week on bus fares) but every single day I nearly get killed.

Cars and taxis and (to a lesser extent buses) appear to own the road and the air. I was a London driver until October last year and now the thought of driving a car disgusts me. Let's create a healthy safe London and ban cars from the congestion zone altogether! Alternatively we could create more cycle-only cycle routes.

💬 Scintillate Rich

I too used to be a cyclist in London. I gave up on the morning slog to work on the tube – halving my travelling time, getting some much needed exercise and letting the pennies stay in my bank account for a few hours longer – until I got knocked off my bike and ended up in hospital with a fractured skull.

(Please note: Chelsea and Westminster hospital is a great hospital – if ever you need one – but no-one ever seems to know where it is or how to get there and so don't expect any visitors while you're gasping your last breath.)

Anyway, I don't cycle any more. Bloody eye-witnesses won't go to court, even though they saw the whole thing and gave a statement to the police. Why? Even the copper said I had a cast-iron case and it was definitely the driver's fault – so now I don my trainers and hotfoot it to work – and oh boy, is it hot at the moment!

So cyclists beware – the drivers of London are psychos and watch out especially for a guy driving a white transit van (what else?) who gets his kicks knocking cyclists off their bikes!

💬 Tizzy

You are absolutely right, cycling in London is horrible and dangerous and very, very scary. A good friend of mine is still in hospital, having been knocked down weeks ago. With that said, I still cycle to work most days. The more people who cycle, the safer London's streets will be. We cannot give in to the evil drivers. We need to resist their intimidation tactics! I urge you to get back on your bike and show them you are not afraid!

💬 Abi

MAN, VAN

I can't drive and don't want to ask a friend to take a day off to drive a van for me, so what I am looking for is a reliable, helpful but cheap human with a van – anyone know where I can find one? I'm in Tooting.

💬 Nancy

I recently used a South African bloke called Charlton who was cheap (£30/hr all in) and bloody strong in that he picked up my moped and threw it in the back of his lorry single-handedly. I think the original advert was on www.gumtree.com.

🗩 **littlejon**

Try Alternative Transport Services: www.alternativetransportservices.co.uk.

And don't be put off by the '96-esque website. I had to move at exceedingly short notice last year, found them online and booked a van and driver for later that day. Both turned up when they said, and the driver was as helpful and unsurly as could ever be hoped. I was done so quickly and easily that I'm amazed that I've not recommended them to anyone before this. Ring them on 08000 131211.

🗩 **Josh**

BEND

Why is the Blackwall Tunnel not straight? Coming from the south it has two bends to the left of approximately 45 degrees, followed by two to the right, then another to the left. I can understand tube tunnels having to bend to avoid foundations, underground rivers etc., but surely something that runs under the Thames should have been easy to build in a straight line. Anyone know about tunnel engineering?

🗩 **Tikki**

Back in Victorian times when the Blackwall and Rotherhithe tunnels were first built, the traffic going through was of the horse and cart variety. Apparently, when a horse goes

into a tunnel and sees light at the other end, it has
a tendency to bolt for that opening. So, bends were put
at each end to prevent this, allowing the riders to control
the horses and to prevent the good people of Rotherhithe,
Limehouse, Blackwall and Greenwich getting trampled on
a regular basis.

The reason that the second Blackwall Tunnel (1960s) is
bendy is not to do with foundations, which wouldn't have
been a problem, but more to do with avoiding contaminated
ground from a gas works. Swerving to miss it meant not
putting tunnel workers' lives at risk and avoiding a very
costly ground clear up. Hope this helps.

💬 **Oz**

SCOOTER

**Every time I walk around the West End, particularly
Soho, virtually every parked motorbike/scooter
I see has its number plate deliberately obscured,
more often than not with a plastic carrier bag. What's this all
about? As a biker, am I missing a trick here?**

💬 **Judetheobvious**

Traffic wardens aren't allowed to tamper with offending
vehicles, so if you ingeniously cover up the number plate
then they are pretty powerless to issue a parking ticket
when the scooter/bike is parked on the pavement.

Watch out though – policemen are allowed to tamper,
so if they get together with the traffic wardens then there's
hell to pay. Park in Soho and it's safety in numbers – they
can't do everyone can they?!

💬 **BikerBoz**

The answer is simple – it allows you to park illegally without being ticketed. Traffic wardens and parking attendants are not allowed to move any part of the vehicle, so if you obscure the number plate with a bag, they can't ticket you as they don't have your number.

So any bike with the plate covered is likely to be breaking some kind of parking rule. Surely only a matter of time before they change the rules (and I suspect not displaying a plate is illegal for other reasons), but for now, park on...

💬 **Christophe**

Well matey, you are kind of missing out on the great number plate cover up, in that bikers seem to think that by obscuring their number plate when parked in a slightly dodgy location, they will not be able to receive a parking ticket for said bike.

This is because traffic police aren't allowed to remove whatever is covering the plate. Unfortunately, this is a foolhardy notion, as all the traffic police have to do is get the registration number off your tax disc, which should be clearly displayed. If it isn't you are liable to a big fine... I know, I went to court over it and lost.

💬 **disgruntledworseoffbiker**

RIVER

After staring drunkenly at the river through the bottom of a pint of lager whilst wondering how to get home from the South Bank to Putney, I was struck by London's lack of water taxis, I know that there are meant to be a couple here and there which you can catch if your father's father was a water boatman and had remembered to thoughtfully book one for you in advance several decades ago, but what about high powered inflatable boats which can be summoned in minutes by mobile?

This would put a bit of life into the river and have the added bonus that if you throw up on your fast and furious ride home it's easy to wash away! So, this is a call to all of those frustrated, unhappy city chaps with a bit of ready cash and a hankering to own an armada of rubber boats – get out there!

Kenton

I used to get the boat to and from work every day when I worked in town a couple of years back. I live on the Isle of Dogs, so I used to get a bus to Westferry Circus (the CW pier is alongside *Jamie's*, *Gaucho Grill*, *Scu-Zi* etc), and then a boat to London Bridge. It also stopped at Rotherhithe, MastHouse Terrace, Tower Bridge, Bankside, Blackfriars and Savoy Embankment. The one I used to get was operated by Collins River Cruises (www.thamesclippers.com). They operated only one boat when I used to get it, but I understand they have more now and are consequently a lot more frequent.

It was a cracking way to get to work. You were guaranteed a seat and you had a great view all the way there. And they would serve drinks, but only if they weren't too busy. On not-too-busy days I'd have a glass of orange juice on the way in, and a bottle of beer and a copy of the *Standard* (which they also sold on the boat) on the way home. 16 minutes each way on the river, plus a five minutes bus ride on the IoD and a two minute walk by London Bridge. Marvellous stuff.

💬 Oz

And finally

RELAX

As I tucked into my new commuting book, *The Art of Living* by that Dalai Lama bloke, I was plagued by a hovering nightmare that is all too common on a Monday morning, namely, 'Uh-oh, this journey to the City is gonna be more crowds, couriers and cold weather'.

A couple of pages later I arrived at London Bridge, got off the train and then practically floated all the way to Moorgate without a hint of stress. And all because of a book.

What I want to know, dear reader, is whether your particular public transport pulp does the same for you every so often? Kinda take you by surprise?

💬 BeeG

On The Road by Jack Kerouac did the same for me. Relaxing and motivating at the same time. Which is clever. These days however, I drive to work and so I'm spared the horrors of public transport and walking to work across Croxley Moor in the pouring rain/freezing cold.

💬 Sudonim

I have discovered the best commuter read ever. I was given *The Sexual Life of Catherine M* by Catherine Miller for Christmas by my best mate, who challenged me to read it brazenly on the tube without blushing. Quite a challenge this one! It's possibly the rudest book I've ever tried to read first thing in the morning. The last time a book felt this naughty was *Forever* by Judy Blume. My tube rage has completely disappeared, as I'm too busy sniggering behind the pages like a teenager. My journey time seems to have halved as I spend most of my time trying to hide the pages from the old dears sat next to me. Then I turn up to work with a bit of a healthy flush and everyone says how well I look.

💬 KT

I'm glad that dipping into slightly, um, sexually upfront books of a morning helped you, KT. That means that so far we have the soothing, philosophical tones of the Dalai Lama and Catherine Miller's pure raunch to recommend to LBL punters for a stress-free commute. Any more for any more?

I'm tucking into *Nelson Mandela: in his own words* right now – interesting, if a bit gushing so far.

💬 Billy Gee

Places

Confused by London postcodes? Struggling with the correct pronunciation of Holborn? Looking for a culture fix? Or a central London swimming pool? Or the best place in the Capital to learn kick boxing? Or the best place to buy a custom-designed wedding ring? Then this is the section for you. Because going out is the new... well, you know.

Lay of the land

MISSING

I've lived in South London all my life and the one thing that has always been a niggling issue in the back of my mind is a lack of a 'South' in London postal codes. There is N, NE, E, SE, SW, W, NW and no 'S'.

Could this be part of some World War Two government scheme to confuse the Germans if they ever invaded? Or is there another reason?

F

London gained 10 lettered postcodes in 1856 as a result of a suggestion by Sir Rowland Hill. These were W, SW, S, SE, E, NE, N, NW, EC and WC. In 1866 NE and E were merged on the recommendation of one Anthony Trollope, then a surveyor with the Post Office, as NE was no longer considered viable. In 1868 S was merged with SW and SE. NE and S were not, however completely dispensed with, in order that they might be used elsewhere as Newcastle and Sheffield did not gain postcodes until the early 1930s.

Interestingly, the numbered districts were not introduced until 1917 and were designed to aid the women who had taken over the jobs of the postmen during the war. They did not have the years of knowledge regarding addresses that the men, who had been delivering mail for decades, had accumulated. The numbered districts may appear randomly placed but actually, after N1, SW1 or W1 etc., which were the district office locations, they are allocated alphabetically according to sub-district.

While I have been able to discover why NE was abolished, I have been unable to find out why S was merged with SW and SE, despite many hours of Googling at the expense of my employer. If anyone knows I would be grateful to be able to sleep at night again.

For those of you who may care to learn more about the exciting world that is the London postcode, most of this information was cribbed from:

www.royalmailgroup.com/heritage/downloads/infosheet_4.pdf.

⌨ Rob

BRIDGE

I was down at *The Bulls Head* by Barnes Bridge and fell in love with the area – the lapping water, the tranquil streets, the non-city feel... Put me out of my misery – it's hugely expensive to live there isn't it? By hugely expensive I mean more than £200k for a one bed flat large enough to swing a cat in.

⌨ kljazz

The village end of Barnes is pretty idyllic, bordered by a curve in the Thames with a duck pond that leads onto Barnes Common. There's a traditional high street that includes many boutique (read 'expensive') shops and exquisite (again, read 'expensive') restaurants.

There's a real feeling of community among its residents, most of whom are professional couples and families (and a clutch of B, C and D-list slebs). It's not one for those who want a lively nightlife in the locale, a bit of bohemia, some student digs, a cheap caff round the corner, or a quick route into central London because none of those things is to be found.

You also have to put up with having the Heathrow landing path overhead several days a month. But is it hugely expensive? Oh, let me count the ways. Barnes is by long-standing tradition one of the most expensive areas in the UK. You must have a car (no tube, precious little train service, no supermarket or large store of any description), so you rely on Richmond, Sheen, Putney and Hammersmith for the majority of your consumer goods. The council tax bills have to be seen to be believed. And as for property prices, it's a very settled area, so amongst the few available at any time you'd be hard pushed to find any flat for under 200K even without cat-swinging, as more average flat prices are now 250-400K.

Those of you with a heart condition or of nervous disposition, look away now. Terraced houses are over 500K, semis over 800K (and some run over 1M). I won't even bother to tell you about detached houses. But having said that, if you love a quiet, characterful, family-oriented village setting, if you don't mind having little choice in the way of public transport, and if you can wangle a big fat mortgage, it's a wonderful area.

💬 **Lady Barnes**

Lady Barnes has it on the nose. I've just moved back to SW13 after a few years away (a failed relationship needed the balm of Barnes, although I doubt I'll find the new love of my life while browsing in the Fine Cheese Shop) and it's great to be back. It calls itself a village and undoubtedly justifies it. And it is definitely not the place to live if you're looking to cut costs.

While the bus services are tolerable (so long as you want to go to Hammersmith) and the trains reasonable (infrequent from the central Barnes Bridge station, much more frequent from the less accessible Barnes station) this only serves to underline its exclusivity.

And the pond is back and refilled, so roll on the summer and lazing around with a pint from the *Sun*. Or the *Red Lion*. Or the *Bulls Head*. Or the *White Hart*. Oh the choices.

Actually, what am I saying? Part of its charm is that no-one thinks they can afford it so don't even try – and that's fine by us.

🗨 No Pikeys

ROE GOOD?

Does anyone know what Roehampton is like to live in? I want to rent a one-bed flat (sick of sharing). I work in Waterloo, so South-West London seems like a good bet, but I can't afford the crazy prices of Putney, Richmond, Wandsworth, etc. Roehampton seems like a little oasis of cheapness in the middle of it all, and there seems to be a supply of one-bed flats in not-very-fashionable ex-council tower blocks with balconies overlooking Richmond Park.

So far so good, but as a single girly, I'd like to know about the safeness of the area before I move in. Transport links look a bit crap, so would I be safe(ish) walking back from Barnes or Putney at night? Are there night buses that aren't full of knife-wielding maniacs?

All info appreciated.

🗨 Kate

It's not too bad, depending on the area. Roehampton village itself is quite nice, a mostly happy mingling of the estate

16-year-old with seven kids, and the student from the Uni there. Many old folks, a few hard-cases. The N74 is a good night bus. The transport links are fine, really – the train from Barnes to Waterloo via Clapham Junction and Vauxhall gets you into town in 20 minutes.

You'd be best off looking for somewhere around the bottom of Dover House Road for proximity to the station, but there are buses (265 and 33, I think) that go from Roehampton to Barnes station. If I were you, which, being a strapping 28-year-old male, I'm clearly not, I wouldn't walk from Barnes station at night – it's poorly lit, non-residential and goes through some potentially dicey estates.

And walking from Putney to Roehampton at any time is quite a trek, especially after a pina colada or six. But as I said, the buses are not bad at all, no more knife-wielding maniacs than anywhere else. My advice would be to see the flat, assess the location, proximity to decent bus routes (the 430 is the most regular route by far), and decide based on that. It's a decent enough area, generally.

🗩 **McTeague**

I've only ever driven through it, but if you work in Waterloo, Surbiton is a good bet, with loads of direct trains taking about 15 mins. It's not massively pricey, and despite what those who've never been there say, it's actually a decent place to live with plenty of good pubs, some great restaurants and plenty of shopping in Kingston (short walk away). Well worth a look if you fancy being able to walk home in relative peace and quiet.

🗩 **bookemdanno**

Living in Roehampton ain't all that I'm afraid. The reason a lot of accommodation is cheap, is because it is all primarily student housing. The ex-council estates you mentioned aren't exactly welcoming, they have their fair share of trouble, and students are always told never to walk alone, especially at night.

I used to live there while studying at the Uni and couldn't wait to get out (into the much more friendly Putney). There are night buses that service Roehampton, but Barnes train station is a brisk 20 minute walk away, and you can't really walk to Putney station, and there are no tubes nearby. Everywhere has its unpleasant side, but I would honestly pay a little bit more and live nearer Putney or Wandsworth.

💬 **Benners**

I live near Roehampton and there are parts where I definitely wouldn't feel safe as a single girl at night. It does have a reputation for not being safe as I know some take away delivery companies won't deliver there. There are lots of buses but I've never used them so couldn't comment on the calibre of passengers! It would be worth visiting to see as I hate to condemn anywhere, especially as they are trying to improve the area. I know Majestic have just built a new wine warehouse and there is a 24-hour *Sainsbury's* at the petrol station.

💬 **Vero**

Roehampton is a safe area, but you have to entertain yourself elsewhere as (correct me if I'm wrong), it totally lacks decent boozers and caffs. Like anywhere else, you really must avoid walking across Barnes Common or Putney Common/Heath at night. I would not recommend trying to walk home to Roehampton from Barnes, which is cut off by obstacles such as the river and the common, unless you walked down to Mortlake and back up.

You can always visit the marvellous restaurants, pubs, cinemas, etc., in East Sheen and Richmond instead, which would keep you on the right side of the commons and would mean you walk home along well-lit roads. And there are lots of buses that serve that route along the Upper Richmond Road after kicking-out time.

The only other crime hotspot is if you have a car, don't park it (especially overnight) along the access roads to Barnes railway station that cut across the commons. Only clueless suburbanites park there so they can hop onto the Waterloo-bound trains, chuckling to themselves as they think they've beaten the system. Invariably the laughter turns to tears when they return in the evening to find every single car has had its windows smashed and their whole collection of Ocean Colour Scene CDs have been stolen.

🗨 **Mister Bob Dobelina**

BETTER LEYT?

I was thinking about moving to Leyton/Leytonstone as this seems to be more in my price range than places a little further in. However I know next to nothing about the area and could do with some tips and advice.

🗨 **Jenn**

I've lived in Leytonstone for three years now and can thoroughly recommend it. The high street shops are a bit pap but you can get most things you need. It's a very friendly area, with some pretty good pubs. There's enough decent ones to do a good pub crawl on a Saturday night. The clientele in the pubs are generally in the 20–30 range but every now and again your get the obligatory smelly old bloke perving at the ladies. I've found it to be safe at night too. Transport links are superb as it's close to both the M11 (going north) and the A12 (going south through the Blackwall Tunnel). Using the Central line it takes about 15 mins to get to Bank which is a real bonus too. Lastly, it's very close to 'trendy' Wanstead if you want decent restaurants and posh bars. And best of all, it's close to acres of parkland (Epping Forest), superb for cycling about on a summers evening without car fumes clogging up your lungs. Can't comment for Leyton though – I think it's a bit dodgier and smellier.

⌨ **Leytonstone Boy**

I noticed something very odd the other night. On the northern side of Fournier Street, off Brick Lane, there are two large wooden doors padlocked together and a letterbox in one of them at a height of about eight feet.

I snuck a look through a crack in the wood and saw what appeared to be a private street. It was dark so I couldn't make out much but there were definitely some small houses at the far end and several coats of arms and sculpture busts hanging on the street walls at the near end. It was like looking into Narnia or something.

⌨ **Solace**

A good place for you to be is Walthamstow. It's a 20-minute train ride to Liverpool Street, a 30-minute tube to Oxford Circus and it's easy to get out of town with quick links to the M11, North Circular and M25. Buses are superb too.

The choices for evening entertainment aren't too spectacular, but the village has a couple of lovely pubs, restaurants and a deli that more than make up for it. Also, Highbury and Islington just 20 minutes away on the tube.

🖵 daveski

I read this every week and never know anything, until now! Regarding a good place in North London that is easy to get to from Liverpool Street, might I suggest Walthamstow? Prices are really reasonable. It is close to Walthamstow Central tube and Leyton if you don't mind a longish walk (40 minutes) or a shortish bus ride (ten minutes). There is overground to and from Liverpool Street, and buses to many different parts of London including London Bridge, Holborn, Wood Green and Essex (should you want to venture there). There are two *Tesco*'s plus an *Asda* and a *Sainsbury*'s a bit further away. Also, Leyton Mills is opposite Leyton station, and that has a HUGE *Asda*. No borough would be complete without a market, and Walthamstow Market is the longest in London, and many a bargain can be found there. Also has a shopping mall and the usual variety of fast food/takeaway type things. You really can't go wrong.

Only thing would be that council tax is pretty steep, so it is better to find a flat that includes council tax in the rent. I found mine in *LOOT* and it has made so much difference. Good luck finding somewhere!

🖵 The Secret Person

Leyton and Leytonstone are a bit rough for a girly living on her own but if you go to Snaresbrook or South Woodford it is a lot nicer (one or two stops further out on the Central

Line). It is also a lot more green as that is where Epping Forest starts. There are some nice bars and restaurants in South Woodford/Wanstead too and it's quite a young area.

💬 **Small Fi**

How about Stoke Newington, Bethnal Green or London Fields? All within easy reach of Liverpool Street and the centre of town, however you may have to rid yourself of the desire to be near a tube and you'll need to remember that buses are cool if you plump for Stoke Newington – but it's worth it.

💬 **Magpie**

I have just moved from Hampstead and bought my first flat in Walthamstow, next to Leyton. My two-bed flat with garden cost half what my mate just paid for a tiny one-bed in Hammersmith.
Tube stations are Walthamstow Central and Blackhorse Road on Victoria line and trains are Walthamstow Central, Queen Street, St James Street. I work in the West End and it takes around 25 minutes to Oxford Circus. The advantage is that you can always get a seat in the morning as Walthamstow Central is at the end of the line. Alternatively, you can take the overland straight into Liverpool Street from the same station. This takes around 20–30 minutes.

The whole area is under regeneration at the moment including a new bus depot, which will incorporate a new tube entrance, plans for a new library and lots of new housing and refurbishment.

It's close to the North Circular and Waltham Forest, and it's a 20-minute drive to Camden. The market is fantastic and there are the usual suspect chain stores in the shopping centre.

The options for stuff to do aren't that great just yet as they are battling to re-open the cinema and there are loads of 'old man boozers' but recently the first 'bar' opened and we hope more to follow. However, it's not far from the West End as I said, or you can go to Wood Green if you have transport which isn't far, for chain pubs and cinemas and more shops. However, there are 24-hour shops selling everything including booze and late night curries etc.

In terms of safety, it's probably no worse than anywhere else and I certainly haven't heard as many sirens as I did living in Hampstead.

House prices fluctuate between streets. Expect to pay more for the streets off the high street and almost ridiculous prices in 'The Village' (Upper Walthamstow). Most properties are ex-Warner and are purpose-built maisonettes from just after the turn of the century. They are very roomy with high ceilings and most have shared gardens. I just bought one and love it to bits. Good luck.

💬 phatflaresblack

PRONOUNCE

How do you pronounce 'Holborn'? Is it HoLborn or HOborn? It would help settle a rather raucous argument.

💬 Fred

'The 'l' in Holborn is not pronounced when referring to the London place name' says my pronunciation guide. I agree, and I live nearby.

💬 Galatea

I work on High Holborn, and I'm sure that pronouncing the 'l' is akin to pronouncing the 'g' in tagliatelle, i.e. wrong.

💬 Gorilla

An empty-headed, self-righteous and thoroughly irritating person I know pronounces it as 'HOborn'.

Therefore, in an effort to distance myself utterly from her, I'd say the other one.

💬 Damian

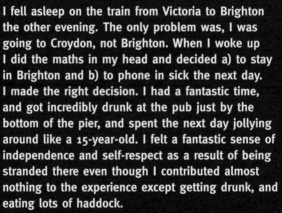

I fell asleep on the train from Victoria to Brighton the other evening. The only problem was, I was going to Croydon, not Brighton. When I woke up I did the maths in my head and decided a) to stay in Brighton and b) to phone in sick the next day. I made the right decision. I had a fantastic time, and got incredibly drunk at the pub just by the bottom of the pier, and spent the next day jollying around like a 15-year-old. I felt a fantastic sense of independence and self-respect as a result of being stranded there even though I contributed almost nothing to the experience except getting drunk, and eating lots of haddock.

💬 Malcolm Barnes

Culture

MUCH ABOUT HISTORY

I'm always hearing about the general intellectual meltdown in society these days, so I was wondering how often your well-informed, icecream nostalgic readership manage to go to museums. Not art galleries or anything like that; most people I know have trooped round *Tate Modern* a few times more than is good for them. But actual proper museums. How popular is the *V&A* with today's Internet types? How about the *Science Museum*? Does anyone else enjoy going there to stare at that lovely blue wall if they're a bit hung over? Or, how about the *Museum of Garden History*? Now there's a little gem. I think they're lush. They're dead quiet as well, which is just great if you ask me.

⌨ Willis

I find myself between jobs at the moment and carrying on with some American lass who needs diversions so we did the Museum trail (culture at bargain prices, who can beat it?).

I'd forgotten how much fun museums can be, even better when you're grown up and not under the supervision of teachers/responsible adults. Of course by the fourth day of standing in front of another ancient lump of rock it was wearing a bit thin but there's some really great stuff happening that you'll only really find out about once you begin to immerse yourself. And of course looking at the Indian/Polynesian temple carvings can give you a few fine hints for the night ahead too. I love culture I do...

⌨ Dan

I hate museums. Their only function is to plunge your childhood into abject boredom. Sorry, but at no point between the ages of seven and 15 did I ever have the desire to stare at dinosaur bones for a day or to walk around a mocked-up trench, complete with realistic smells. Yet I was forced to. Which is why, if I ever get the opportunity, I will bomb the shit out of the *Natural History Museum* (hopefully taking out the *Science Museum* and *V&A* at the same time), Duxford, and the Greenwich peninsula (levelling the *Maritime Museum* and *Toy Museum* and, praise the Lord, the *Cutty Sark*).

🗨 Alex

GUTS

Has anyone got up the guts to actually enter the Feliks Topolski free museum on Sutton Walk on the South Bank? I walk past it every day to work but am too scared to go in. It looks like a Goth nightclub and I've never seen anyone come out of it. Do you know any more about it? Is it good? What's the point of it then?

🗨 Davey Chells

According to the snazzy leaflet I have to hand, *Memoir of the Century* is artist Feliks Topolski's visual record of the personalities and the social and political events of the 20th Century that he witnessed during a lifetime spent travelling the globe. *The Memoir*, a unique 600-foot long 12- to 20-foot high panoramic painting which Topolski began in 1975, is the continuation and final outcome of these activities'.

The railway arch in which this memoir is situated seems to leak permanently which seems to add to the effect of a somewhat shabby, mysterious underworld. Working close by, I see endless people peering in, hesitating at the entrance, wondering whether if they enter, they will ever emerge again. It is kept going by Tolpolski's son who has a studio nearby. Incidentally, they carry on the very quaint tradition of cheese and wine at the studio – a kind of get to know the artists. I stop short at making a judgement on the 'exhibition' suffice to say many of my colleagues have thought that turning it into a Goth bar might be more entertaining.

💬 **niceday**

I have been in the *Feliks Topolski Museum*, and all I can say is that it used to be a much more famous attraction than it is now. The official name is *The Memoir of the Century*, and more can be found on www.felikstopolski.com/memoir.htm. It is worth visiting, if only to say how you've been there and you don't know anyone else who has.

💬 **Gentleman Loner**

You must pluck up the courage to have a look at this. Topolski was an amazing artist who lived and worked there and his work was created and gathered there and still remains there. When he was alive, he had 'drop-in evenings' when anyone who wanted to could drop in and have a chat with him. I did it once. He was very interesting but his work is incredible. He called his work collectively a *Memoir of the Century* and he energetically created his responses to what was going on in the 20th Century. It's not scary but it is fun.

💬 **Billy**

WORTH

Having lived in London all my life I feel I should actually make an effort and see what we have to offer. Does anyone know of some good museums, galleries, buildings of interest, exhibitions etc., etc., that are not a complete rip-off to get into, but are well worth a visit?

◻ **Feebs**

The London open house weekend in September is always a £3.75 well spent. Buy the guide here http://www.londonopenhouse.org and then spend the weekend getting in free to houses all over London that you wouldn't normally be allowed in.

The houses range from grand Crown Estate buildings to architects and keen DIYers who own swanky pads. We had a very entertaining time visiting one of the 'dancing' houses near St Pancras where we were taken on a tour of a dance school, interspersed with performances of contemporary dance (although I don't think they found our uncontrollable fits of childish giggling as amusing as we found their silent 'getting buggered up against a wall and swinging round a lampost' dance).

◻ **Harri**

Have a look at LondonFreeList (www.londonfreelist.com). It lists all the events and attractions in London that you don't need much money to go to. They are all either free or cost no more than £3 maximum.

◻ **Abi**

Feebs, there is a great Museum that has only been open for a year. *The Museum* in Docklands is about the 2000-year history of the London ports, river and people. There were loads of interactive displays, touch screens and videos. The staff were amazing, not like those sitting in the corner bunch that you normally see in places like that. Best of all it cost £5 for a whole year's ticket! It also massive, it took me two visits.

The children's gallery is really good fun, only they wouldn't let the 30-somethings on the soft play area. It has also a great quayside bar – 1802. Its over at West India Quay, a bit hard to find but you can get there on the DLR. Website is www.museumindocklands.org.uk. Go find it!

🗨 **Thepnut**

I can recommend the *Time Out Book of London Walks* as a great way to see some of the capital's sights, particularly those a bit off the beaten track. The walks I've done include pub stops and haven't been too strenuous. A really enjoyable way to while away a sunny day and spend some quality time with those who matter without having to part with too much cash – just don't get stuck at the first pub you come to!

🗨 **Lillibet**

GEORGE

I've been reading *London* by Edward Rutherford, which follows fictional families throughout London's history. And besides a slight loss of interest throughout the middle ages it's a bloody good read. Living south of the river most of my life I've learnt loads about the old town from the book but don't really know many of the areas it talks about. This is all changing

however. Thanks to a combination of living here permanently
again, reading Rutherford's book, subscribing
to London by London and listening to Robert Elms I've just
gone mad on finding great little corners of the city.

Anyway, there is a pub in the book which the characters
have been frequenting since the early 1300s and it's as
much a part of the book as any of the fictional families are.
And that's pretty much what I thought it was; just one of
the fictional places. So, I was chatting to a girl at a party
last Sunday and she tells me that her brother is the manager
of the second oldest pub in London right near London
Bridge. I stared back at her in bleary-eyed surprise when
she even told me it's called *The George*. Needless to say
I went looking for the place and loved it.

Great old pub. I can practically see Shakespeare sitting
in a dark corner. (If you moved the damn fruit machine out
the way. Maybe put Shakespeare in the other corner). Nice
pub, beautiful old building. I can't stand these crappy high
street bars anymore. They're everywhere.

Anyway I was giddy with excitement at finding the place
(Left out of London Bridge tube away from the bridge) and
just wanted to share it with someone. This seemed like
a good start. So can anyone point me to any other slightly
hidden, nice little old man pubs that won't all stop what
they're doing and glare at me as I walk in the door?

🖵 **Monkavich**

I read Edward Rutherford's *London* just after I moved here
a few years ago. I'd recommend it to anyone moving to the
capital – it's a fascinating history lesson as well as a great
novel. Sure, there's a few liberties taken with some historical

events and figures, but it's forgivable when it teaches you so much about how London grew over the last 2000 years from being a small fishing community into the city we now know. And there are some wonderful characters too.

Be warned though. It's a monster of a book, and it'll take a while to read. But at least it'd be a relief to see more of you on the tube reading *London* than Harry Bloody Potter.

💬 **SJW**

In answer to Monkavich's request for hidden public house gems, might I recommend *The Seven Stars* at 53 Carey Street, WC2? This fantastic 17th Century delight is nestled in the bosom of London's legal-land. Sadly, extreme wine consumption during previous visits prevents me from recalling the precise location, but it's up the road from the utterly charmless *Wetherspoons*.

Run by the 'charismatic' Roxy Beaujolais with her love of fine French foods (including the suspicious looking sausages of *Blackadder* fame) *The Seven Stars* is staffed almost exclusively by buxom foreign imports who go down a treat with ale-drenched barristers making a second home of the bar stools, whilst their wives sit at home wondering whether to start having sex with the late night meat manager at their local Waitrose.

For your personal protection, should any rodents cut up rough, the premises are prowled by a Master Tom Paine, a feline whose 'Weapons of Mouse Destruction' are lovingly depicted in one of the many dusty prints lining the 400-year-old walls. This pub is one of a handful of buildings to survive the Great Fire of London in 1666. Its only downside therefore is its compact nature, as peeps were titchier in them days.

Maybe LBL readers could club together and open up a

rival parlour in the vacant lot next door to give old Roxy Beaujolais a run for her Euros. I suggest we call it *Poxy Chardonnay's* and staff it with resting actresses who fell off the *Footballer's Wives* casting couch.

💬 **Lalalondon**

I think *The George* is a bit overrated to be honest, but it's better than an *All Bar One*, so let's not be too critical. There's a fine line between good proper pubs serving nice beer and CAMRA olde-worlde reification replete with Real Ale Twats. But they're out there.

As a starter, can I suggest *The Olde Mitre* (Ely Place, Hatton Garden) or the *Cheshire Cheese* on Fleet Street. Then there's the *Blackfriar* near Blackfriars, handily enough.

But the beauty is in the exploration. For a handy guide, visit www.fancyapint.com or www.beerintheevening.com. Much less useful (but included in a completist vein) is www.pubs.com.

Quizzers could visit www.quizlist.com and sports fans could visit www.sportspubs.com. There's a world of pub information out there, and like all such guides, treat them as a guide, not a bible. They provide basic information, which should be taken with a pinch of salt as it's only one view; you might love the pubs they hate and vice-versa. Though if you disagree with the review for the *Punch and Judy*, you should be shot.

So, explore the joys of London's boozers — you have nothing to lose but your liver.

💬 **Dave**

Out of interest *The George* was where plays were first per-
formed in London and where Shakespeare took his inspira-
tion for building the *Globe*. It is now owned by the National
Trust. Anyway, all the balconies around the outside are like,
well, the balconies and levels in the *Globe*. Also, I happen
to randomly know that as one of the oldest pubs in London,
it was around when there were tolls people had to pay
to enter the City of London. *The George* was originally one
of the last stops before the tolls, which they used to close
late at night. People who were too late to enter the City
usually ended up having to sleep at *The George*, and that
is what the balconies were first used for. Sort of similar to
congestion charges today...

  P.S. Another interesting pub find is *Mistress P's* in
Clapham. Tucked away in the Old Town, it has so far failed
to attract highlighted blonde lovelies and estate agents that
populate most of the area. Gives out free chips, bingo com-
petitions and cheap beer. What more could you ask for?

💬 **Pretty Polly**

Despite the seemingly endless onslaught of corporate chain
pubs and bars, there are still many great pubs in London
that are distinctive, cultural, ooze character or are of quality.
You could start at the *Market Porter*, a pub just around the
corner from *The George*. Although not as old as *The George*,
it still has a sense of culture and interest about it.

  Apparently, this pub owes its abnormally early licence
to its proximity to the wonderful Borough Market with its
thirsty early morning market workers. I have never managed
to get up that early to find out if the licence still exists.
Does anyone know? It's a pub that takes pride in serving
many different English beers from small to medium producers.

I have tried many different styles including porters, stouts, milds, golden ales, light ales, bitters, India Pale Ales, and fruit ales (I could go on), though not necessarily in one session. I have even heard that you may get impromptu acoustic or folk musical sessions there, but again I've never witnessed this. Has anyone?

Other good pubs include the haunted '*Grenadier*', tucked away in Wilton Row, Belgravia. Here you can try its supposedly 'famous' Bloody Marys if you are suffering from a hangover. If you are a fan of extravagant Victorian decorations, there is the *Salisbury Tavern* or maybe the *Dog and Duck* in Soho. If you fancy a bewildering range of beers, then there is the *Jerusalem Tavern* in Farringdon. Or if you like a lazy day by the river, try the *Prospect of Whitby* (or the Town of Ramsgate) in Wapping. A noose hanging over the river serves as a reminder that they used to hang people here.

I could go on and on as I have spent many an enjoyable time finding and drinking in such places. Just go there before they become a *McDonald's*, a *Starbucks* or a chain pub.

🗩 **Heed**

The Palm Tree. Mile End tube station, turn left, under the big bridge, right-hand side of the road, do a right down the little alley outside the *Globe*, down the stairs, onto the towpath (this is getting good,) about three hundred metres north, *The Palm Tree* sits in splendid isolation in the middle of nowhere. It's one of the best pubs in the world and, just to make it interesting, I'm not going to tell you why – I don't see why I should give away all my secrets. Just come along on a Saturday night.

🗩 **Joe**

I like the sound of that pub in Mile End. It's nice to be rewarded for the effort, I think. All rubbish pubs are on main drags, and all the nice ones are tucked away. Which brings me to my suggestion... down near the river in between Putney and Wandsworth, under the railway bridge off Putney Bridge Road, is a great place called *The Cat's Back*. It's a real remnant of '60s West London bohemia, with chaises longues, big kitsch photos of Elvis, Audrey Hepburn and other sorts, and mad old men doing funny knees-up dancing to reggae. Well, there was once.

💬 **Willis**

Things to do

SWIM

Does anyone know where I can go for a lunchtime swim in Covent Garden? I don't want to join a gym as I am already a member near where I live – and as you know, gym fees aren't cheap. Any ideas?

💬 **Aquagirl**

There's the *Oasis* swimming pool and sports centre at the top of Endell Street where it meets High Holborn. This is an OK pool for the general public to use (it costs the usual £2.90 or so for a swim) and has the added bonus of an outside pool for those brave days when the sun actually shines.

However, I do not advocate the use of the outside one purely for the fact that pervy men from the flats a mere ten metres away can perv at you from their balconies. Stick to indoor swimming. It's fine in the summer though – you blend in with the rest of the crowd (therefore reducing the risk of being singled out by the pervs) and they can get off even more by the fact that *Oasis* allows topless sunbathing on a raised platform area!

💬 **barmaid**

SWIM AGAIN

Non-swimming gent here. Anyone know of somewhere in North London or central London where I can get swimming lessons? One on one or as part of an adult group – either is fine but I'm keen to get past going blue in the shallow end.

💬 **Flapper**

Another non-swimming guy here, who intends to learn sometime soon. Camden Council's *Oasis* leisure centre, between Charing Cross Road and Covent Garden, offers a series of ten lessons for beginners.

💬 **Rich**

Church Farm Swimming Pool, Church Hill Road, East Barnet EN4 8XE, Tel: 020 8368 7070. I had lessons here – it was a small group and good fun. Happy flapping!

💬 **Bankgirl**

I go swimming here: www.aquaterra.org. It's cheap to join and the facilities are decent. They are also a charity, which makes me happier parting with my money, rather than to an ordinary gym and they provide beginner classes or refresher courses.

💬 **madpickle**

SPLASH

Anyone know of anywhere I can play water polo in the Victoria/Westminster/Chelsea area? Haven't played for a few years, so probably crap level. I'd like somewhere that does it at weekends/evenings.

🗨 **Roger roger**

My flatmate used to play a lot and has recommended www.otterwaterpolo.com. As my knowledge about water polo extends no further than admiring pictures of Prince William playing I can't tell you anything more, but hopefully the website will be more informative.

🗨 **Nick Nack**

SQUASH

I refuse to believe this is true, but I can't find a non-members squash club/court/whatever! The only one I have found in London thus far is in Brentford, and given that I need access from the City in the middle of the day, it's not helpful.

So, does anyone know of a good place with squash courts that don't require a £300/year membership, and is fairly central? I don't play that well or that often, but the odd game is great, I'd just rather not have to keep painting red lines on the side of buildings in Whitehall. The rozza from the Met told me next time he'd take my racquet away.

🗨 **Mudge**

I don't play squash, but I know that there are few 'pay as you go' leisure centres near to the City, if not in it. Here are a few that I have found that may be good, they all offer squash facilities and you do not have to join to play.

Britannia Leisure Centre, Hoxton, N1
www.britannia.leisureconnection.co.uk.

Finsbury Leisure Centre, Norman Street, EC1
www.aquaterra.org.

Saddlers Sport Centre, Goswell Road, EC1
020 7040 5060.

Also, check out www.cityoflondon.gov.uk
(and www.westminster.gov.uk) which should list facilities
in the City.

> Finsbury Park spelt backwards is 'krapy rub snif'.
> And before you waste a number of hours, no it
> doesn't work for any other station.
>
> innes

You could head to *LA Fitness* in Mansell Street, nearest tube Aldgate which is a gym, with two or three squash courts (www.lafitness.co.uk). The gym isn't that good, but the squash courts are fine. I hope this helps. I have a similar problem but with tennis courts, and netball courts. Since the demolition of the sports place in Spitalfields, there has been nowhere to play tennis or netball at lunchtimes if you work in the City. Sorry, that is all bar one court in the church courtyard that is booked until 2006. I am afraid this has led me to climb on my soapbox. We wonder why this country has so little in the way of sports stars but surely it is

because we have no facilities and sport is just not seen
as important as building yet another huge office complex.
The demolition of the sports centre at Spitalfields was
a disgrace!

💬 **Curly Wurly**

There's a reasonable set of courts at the *Oasis* sports centre
on the corner of High Holborn and Endell Street (closest
tube Holborn). Morning sessions on weekdays are £3.20 per
half hour. Lunchtime and after work hire is more expensive
but not extortionate – and you certainly don't have to be
a member. The number for booking is 020 7831 1804 but
if you phone when it's busy, don't expect to speak to anyone
for a good ten minutes.

One final thing: apparently the centre has a reputation
as a bit of a scouting ground for persons of a particular
persuasion. Not that this has ever caused a problem but do
look out for the slightly officious sign bearing the legend:
'Inappropriate behaviour will not be tolerated'.

💬 **Weak Serve**

WAVES

**Does anyone know of any kind of surfing club
in London, designed to get us city-dwelling 'lubbers
down to the coast to ride some waves every now
and then? I fancy having a crack at the sport, but would
prefer to get involved with some kind of London set-up, rather
than just turning up in Newquay on my own.**

💬 **Timotheus**

In response to Timotheus's query regarding some kind of
surf club in London, please check www.londonsurfclub.com.

Meeting the last Tuesday of every month. Regular trips to the waves organised, subsidised lessons, parties etc.

💬 Sarong

KITE

**I have had a few kitesurfing lessons and loved it so want to buy some kit and get out on the water.
I'm looking for one or more people to go out with – safety, drinks, sharing transport etc., who are also just starting out and live in London.
So is there anyone out there who fancies going, or knows someone who does? Any leads appreciated.**

💬 Mr Ben

Hi Mr Ben – thought you might want some close-to-London kiting recommendations. A brilliant place to go is Camber Sands in Sussex. It's an enormous beach, it's pretty close to London, there are loads of people around to watch out for each other, and you can take lessons with *Kites On Board* (www.kitesonboard) who are based in Rye, who are great.
Of course at this time of year when the weather is sunny and calm, you may want to head off to Tarifa instead!

💬 Zoz

Power Kiting/Kite Surfing is now a huge sport. The best place to meet like-minded people is on the flexifoil forums (you don't have to fly flexi kites to use this!):
www.flexifoil.com/community/forums.
It is worthwhile checking out the areas you intend to fly as there are now kite restrictions at many places.

💬 Blade Maestro

FIGHT

For some four years (since moving to the mean streets of London in fact), I've been a keen little karataka, gleefully kicking things on a weekly basis but I'm not a nutter, oh no, just protective of my girl bod and fond of martial arts.

Thing is, I've just moved to Acton, which means I now have to either travel an hour across town at rush-hour, or two hours across town on a Sunday morning to get to my club, and whilst dear Mr Miyagi would mourn my lack of commitment, quite frankly this to-ing and fro-ing is killing me.

So tell me, wise ones of the LBL clan, where can I do good karate in West London? Mixed classes are cool, but no kid's stuff as I'm 26 and well past my brown belt (and I find hitting people who are way smaller than me just a bit depressing), I'm also not in this purely for the fighting so no rooms full of tattooed bikers just looking for a rumble if at all possible! I don't mind travelling a bit, but under an hour would be good. Help me please, I'm in danger of losing my pretty biceps!

💬 costumekitten

Costumekitten, my memory's a bit hazy, but there's a place on the UxbridgeRoad at the bottom of Twyford Avenue (between Acton and Ealing Common, near the *Tesco Metro* garage thingy) that does martial arts classes. I think it's called *Twyford Leisure Centre*. They definitely do kickboxing and I think they do karate as well. You can turn up and pay per class and it's for all abilities, ages, etc.

💬 Kate

I can recommend a very good gym in Shoreditch –
www.paragongym.co.uk (nearest tube Liverpool Street or Old
Street). Very friendly bunch of people with plenty of females
too. The instructors seem to like being on telly too
– one's been in a Guinness ad and another one's in a Müller
Light yoghurt ad – which is being shown at the moment.

 Hong Kong Suey

> Apropos of nowt, if you walk on the mud under
> Blackfriars Bridge after half tide or lower, look
> at your feet; you are walking on a carpet of
> horses teeth.
>
> Pretzel

Physical Arts is located at Blackfriars and teaches
mugendo-style kickboxing. The teaching is top class and
the people there are all very friendly. There are classes for
beginners right up to advanced, and the Sensei coaches the
GB WAKO team. Although not cheap as chips, it's worth
every penny! I've been there for nine or ten months now
and it's great. They also have classes in yoga, ju-jitsu, tai chi,
wu shu and fitness and toning classes. Enjoy!

Ninja Angel

Not sure if it's too far out but there is the *Fighting Fit*
kickboxing school on Merton Road near South Wimbledon.
www.fighting-fit.com. They have a ladies only night on
Tuesdays. I haven't tried it myself yet, but am going to once
I get back from travelling.

Clefty

KB Kickboxing (www.kbkickboxing.co.uk) is a good club in central London. It is mostly girls and very keen to get everyone together socially too. They have loads of classes and the teachers are excellent.

💬 K

There's a place in Wimbledon where my friend and I attend kickboxing classes. The beginners class is on a Monday evening and they do a kickboxing workout class on a Wednesday evening. It's a really good workout and also great fun. It costs £5 a lesson but if you are a member it would cost you £34 a month I think and that includes all kickboxing and martial art classes too but don't quote me on that.

The teacher's name is Steve and his contact email is steve@holistic-fitness.net. Good luck and hope to bump into you in a class one day!

💬 **Originalpubgirl**

A LITTLE BIT FRIGHTENING

Does anyone know of a proper kung-fu club or academy within central or North London? Searched the web and have come up with nothing. I really need to get back in shape and it's much more fun than gym! Any help appreciated!

💬 **Sinsita**

Sinsita, the best place is the *Bob Breen Academy* in Hoxton Square which teaches jeet kune do with a smattering of boxing, stickfighting and grappling. Bob has a global reputation as the father of JKD and Filipino arts in Europe, and I've never met a bunch of more well-adjusted, interesting, friendly people in my life!

snow

For 'proper' kung fu, as you put it, I can only recommend Sifu Yap Leong. He is an exponent of Shaolin Fists and Five Ancestors, and is one of the few traditional masters still around. He teaches a small but dedicated class twice a week in Covent Garden, and teaches almost every class personally. He's been teaching in or around Chinatown since the 70s and has been a major figure in Chinatown events, as well as appearing on TV and writing for *Combat magazine*.

The classes include conditioning, forms, practical applications, weapons (like aerobic weight training but more fun) and chi kung (like yoga but with combat application) and are taken seriously but with an informal atmosphere. I have trained with Yap Leong for over five years and, although I've tried others, for me nothing else has come close. Socially, its very friendly and we get to take part in the Chinese New Year and Mooncake Festival demonstrations and lion/dragon dance in Chinatown. Lots of fun. You can come and watch a lesson or two free of charge, or take a trial lesson.

caterpillardriller

Don't know if Battersea is too far for you but you could try the *Tang Lung Combat Academy*. It is run by Sifu George Fitzgerald who trained under Victor Khan (one of Bruce Lee's classmates) in wing chun kung fu. Other class available are ju jitsu, combat sombo and tang lung combat. Read all about it at www.tanglung.org/index.htm.

pedal power

For Kung Fu-type antics you could try www.bobbreen.co.uk – this is the *Bob Breen Academy* in Hoxton Square where you can practice jeet kune do and jun fan gung fu – these were the ones practised by Bruce Lee!

It's great fun and you can do beginner or intermediate courses.

💬 **pesk**

The *Bob Breen Academy* is in Hoxton Square, and although it isn't cheap (£60 a month, including gym membership) you won't find any martial arts place that does a better job of getting you fit and teaching you fighting skills that are actually some use. It's jeet kune do rather than kung fu, but many of the skills are very similar.

💬 **W**

CHI

I'm looking for a tai chi class somewhere near Twickenham (or on a bus route from there). Anyone know of a class for beginners? Preferably late evening or weekends.

💬 **orac**

I have learnt for a year with *Mountain River Tai Chi* run by Keith and I wouldn't hesitate to recommend him. I know he teaches in Richmond and suspect he does a class in Twickenham too; go to www.mountainriver.co.uk for more info.

💬 **Katkin**

Places to go...

ROOM

The other day I went to the new GLA building, partly because I was curious to see where the millions and million of pounds of taxpayers' money had gone, but mainly to check out the view from the top floor. London's Living Room is its official title, and it's even listed as that in reception and the lifts.

However there was a flaw in my plan. London's Living Room isn't actually open to Londoners (of course). I was told by a security guard that the public are banned from entering it, except for four hours on alternate Saturdays as long as it's not being used for something else (such as a cocktail party for Ken's army of highly-paid PR people).

Tim

In response to Tim's note about not being able to get to London's Living Room, I too was very interested in seeing this building. But so was the GLA.

The original design of the building and the use of circular stairs was an attempt by the GLA and its architect to make the GLA more accessible to people like us. When it was first opened it was possible to go to the top and have a look. So what happened? A little thing called security. It seems that no-one thought of this, but recent events and higher states of alert have made them add security (metal detectors) and close the top floor to general admission.

A shame, I know, But not because the GLA didn't try.

Jezter

OK, maybe you can't normally get to the top of the GLA building (and it's ages until the next Open London weekend). But one thing that I think is fantastic in the building is the carpet of the basement-entrance Visitors Centre.

It's an aerial photo of London, with the whole of the M25 area covered. Last Open London day, the place was crowded with people crawling around on their hands and knees, obviously looking for their houses/places of work.
Worth looking in if you're passing.

zeroGravitas

Instead of moaning about London's Living Room being closed for understandable security reasons, why not make the effort to go the GLA website where it tells you the weekend dates when it is open to the public:
www.london.gov.uk/gla/city_hall/weekend_opening.jsp.

Now that wasn't hard, was it?

By the way, it's well worth the effort. The view is amazing, and the chance to walk down the spiral ramp indoors is great as well. It's a bit like the Reichstag in Berlin, but much better.

Jif

TRAWL

I am well aware that this probably comes across as sad and desperate but I'm not. Really. Just disheartened. Can anyone please tell me where normal, relatively intelligent single hetero men go out in South London on the weekend?

I am 29, female and live in Clapham, which is probably half the problem – but it seems that whenever I go out there I am surrounded by smug marrieds. Chelsea is peopled by ex-army chaps in red jeans and sloanes in baseball caps. I have been mugged twice in Wandsworth so not too keen on there and don't really know Brixton at all.

Lots of places on the other side of the river, I know, but as I recently heard that I am meant to be living in a bit of town with the most single men in Europe per square mile, or something, I just wondered where they all were. No dudes or chicks please.

Anonymous singleton

Anonymous singleton – it makes no difference where you go in South London. It's all like that. I'm a boy, in exactly the same situation as you and have never found anywhere for intelligent potential mate-liaisons. But, as a summary, if you're interested, here is a guide to pubs I know and the likelihood of meeting single people:

1) *The Bedford*, Balham: Actually not too bad but invaded by out-of-towners on a weekend. Wednesday night's your best bet.

2) *The Balham Tup*: Good for rugby players/associated girls. And Australians. Maybe not your thing.

3) *Smoke*, near Tooting Bec tube: Bit of a dark horse. Getting more popular and worth a punt. Although not very big and not well designed for easy cross-group interaction.

4) *The Duke of Devonshire*, Clapham South: No chance, despite late licence. Ditto the *Rook and Jackdaw* and *Puzzle* (maybe tiny bit better).

5) *Sand*, Clapham: Nice, but no mingling area so useless for meeting new people.

💬 **Greg**

Sounds as though it's the areas of Clapham that you're frequenting to be honest – there are young men a-plenty in some areas. If you don't want to cross the river to the 'golden mile' (Old Street to Liverpool Street to Bethnal Green) then head either to Wandsworth Road (Indigo regularly pulls them in) or nearer Clapham Common or Clapham North. Sunny afternoons in the *Falcon* or *Sun* beer gardens is easy on the eye. (I'm talking about the *Falcon* on Bedford Road rather than the one at Clapham Junction. Mix them up and it could spoil your sunny afternoon altogether!)

Also – get to know Brixton: *Living* and *Bug Bar* are normally pretty good in the pulling stakes.

💬 **Also Anonymous**

WITH THIS RING

I have recently got engaged to my Assassin Princess but not wanting to make a faux pas and present her with a hideous creation that she would forever resent taking up room on her finger I didn't get her a ring when I popped the question. We want something a little bit different but not too 'ooh look at me I'm different'. Can anyone recommend jewellers that might fit the bill?

The Assassin Prince

Mr Sladey bought my ring from *Autumn and May* in Greenwich Market. Their stuff is looks great and is very reasonably priced. And the staff are nice too.

Sladey

Congraulations on your engagement! My beau and I had exactly the same problem, but don't be put off by the reputation Hatton Garden has for expense and your traditional rocks on a ring type thing. My bloke found the people in most of the shops really helpful and quite willing to discuss the options given the size of his budget. He ended up being able to design me a ring (which is gorgeous – who knew he was so creative?) and it didn't break the bank. I did hear from somewhere that Hatton Garden can actually be cheaper than a lot of regular jewellery shops as you're going straight to the source. Good luck!

Furydoll

I'd recommend having a look at Bond Street antiques market. All the rings there are, well, antiques and so your chances of finding something special and especially impressive are high. My loved one bought me a sapphire and diamond 1940s ring, with platinum settings for £1200. He then buggered off whilst I was on holiday with a mate, but don't let that put you off!

LalaLondon

When we got engaged last year we went to Hatton Garden and were laughed out of every jewellers until we stumbled on *Holt's* (in Hatton Garden). They have all manner of precious/semi-precious stones in all shapes and sizes and will mount them for you in a choice of rings. They made us a unique and really beautiful ring and were really friendly and helpful. And it came to about £160 all in.

Mr and Mrs Smith

I wouldn't rule out Hatton Garden as it isn't over-the-top expensive and the best thing about it is you can negotiate if you find something you like. The other places to look if you want something a bit unique are places like *Jess James* on Newburgh Street or *Jeremy Hoye* on Beak Street – both very nice but can be pricey, or *Dinny Hall* in Islington although they tip the scale from pricey into downright expensive.

But I would definitely say try Hatton Garden first – it is all jewellery shops and besides selling both new and antique rings, they'll always offer you a discount. Add to that some very nice pubs nearby where you can relax when you've finally chosen something and are completely drained by the experience (which you will be – it's quite a trying process).

CJ

For having given birth to our daughter, my husband went to a Clerkenwell Green jeweller (www.dominicwalmsley.com)

who made me a bracelet for about £300 that is unique to me. He does rings too and will design it with the input of you and your Assassin Princess.

🗩 **Kitty**

My fiancé and I were looking for an individual engagement ring that was both unique and inexpensive and we found the perfect place. It is a company called *Bespoke Diamond* and advertise mainly through their website: www.bespokediamond.com.

 With their help, we chose the diamond/precious stones we wanted ourselves and designed the setting ourselves, so the end result was exactly what we wanted and I know that no-one else has the same ring as me! They were also far cheaper than the usual retail outlets as they only buy to order. The email address for enquiries is info@bespokediamond.com. We found them to be extremely helpful and knowledgeable throughout the time we were dealing with them and I highly recommend them – hope you find the same.

🗩 **Rachel**

My friend William Cheshire works just off Hatton Garden but is a much more individual jeweller and works with you to create whatever you have in mind rather than the standard. His site is mainly male jewellery but he has done engagement ring commissions for just about everyone I know and it's a very eclectic set of tastes so he will almost certainly be able to match what you want. www.williamcheshire.com.

🗩 **Gavin**

Why not try a bespoke jeweller? They will make a ring specific to you and your Princess, at a price you specify.

The best I have ever come across is Jane Runchman. She's a really funky and talented jeweller who will make totally one-off rings for a price that suits you. Here's some of her work: www.janerunchman.com.

Then your Princess knows that the ring she has is the only one like that in the world, rather than a run-of-the-mill rock.

💬 **Little Gem**

I recently had a ring made by Karen Gledhill in the Oxo Tower – her partner in the shop (Tony) also does some wonderful designs. If you want something wearable but slightly different I would certainly recomend them. There are about four jewellery shops in the tower so it's well worth a visit.

💬 **radar**

My beloved and I got our rings from a stereotypical old Jewish Eastern European jeweller called Mr Cohen, who has a stall in Covent Garden Market on Saturdays (and, I think, Fridays). He has a range of styles, and is very reasonably priced. To give you a vague idea, the engagement ring (diamond solitaire in platinum) cost £650 compared to well over £1k for similar ones in Hatton Garden.

However, I know you said you don't want a diamond solitaire but he will also custom-make rings. Or you could always make the ring yourself! I know there are classes out there for this (I think it involves spending a Saturday in a workshop) but don't have any details – perhaps somebody else out there knows about it.

💬 **braindead geordie**

Sounds like you and your princess are in a similar situation to what I was in a short while back with my 'noble warrior'.

He, very lovelyly, proposed on a beach, without said ring, as he knew I was a little fussy and 'different'. The problem was, I wanted a ring that looked like an engagement ring, but not just another diamond platinum ring.

We went off to Hatton Garden, which just made me worry because I really didn't like anything. They do have thousands of variations, but they are really just variations on one theme.

We went to *Electric* in South Molton Street, which has jewellery by a variety of different designers and all of it is high quality and interesting work. I saw a couple of designs that I loved for very different reasons, and in the end went for a ring that is recognisably an engagement ring, but is just a little bit unique and special. I've now had it a couple of months, and it still catches my eye when I'm on the tube escalator, or waiting for something, and I think it is so special I get excited about our wedding day to come.

A friend of mine went there too, and liked a ring which was quite a bit out of her price bracket and is now having something similar made by someone in South Africa. So even if you can't afford something, it might just give you ideas of what you want to design and commission yourself.

Another thing to do is to visit jewellery designers in their studios. Basically if you find someone who shares your philosophy and taste, you will find something very special to you both.

Check out Hidden Art at www.hiddenart.com, which lists a lot of jewellery designers. Hope this helps and enjoy. It's a great purchase to be making, and can be most rewarding, just don't let it stress you out.

💬 **Briony**

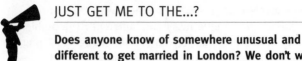

JUST GET ME TO THE...?

Does anyone know of somewhere unusual and different to get married in London? We don't want a big service, just somewhere a bit bizarre and kooky for a (very) few people. Oh and it would be nice if it could be legally binding too.

💬 **Cassius**

My friends got married at *London Zoo*. They have a fairly large ceremony room/dining hall and bar, and the food and service was great. And they have orangutans, lemurs, lizards, penguins, ocelots, giraffes... What more could you want for your wedding day?!

💬 **longjon**

CAFÉ CULTURE

I've been meaning to ask if anyone knows of any German or French cafés in London. They existed in Edinburgh and I used to go regularly when I was an interpreting student just to chat to the many French/German people who would hang out there. They must be around in London too, but I've not heard of any. Anyone know?

💬 **Little G**

I've been trying to learn/improve my French for some time now due to work, and quite a lot of people I know have recommended hanging about at the French Institute in South Kensington (just off Harrington Road). Not only do they have a good cinema (cheaper than the Odeons/UCI too), but there is a little coffee bar full of nice French people. As for German, there is a place called '*Hugo's*' on Exhibition Road, which is sort of connected to the German Institute. It's great there, otherwise there is the institute itself.

💬 mudgewah

Just a quick response to Little G, there is a French bar/café called *Café Kick* in Clarkenwell (www.cafekick.co.uk). It is very popular with the French ex-pat community, and hence a great place to practice your French. As the name suggests, table football is a very important social activity there, so you'd better get some practice in before going... hope you like Pernod/Pastis too!

💬 Kaiser

Anyone who wants to get designer clothes at silly prices should register with Designer Warehouse Sales (www.designerwarehousesales.com), who sell on designers' samples and last season's unsold stuff. They have three-day sales every couple of months or so, just by King's Cross station, stocking all the big names and some less well-known designers. There's a fair bit of 'who the hell would wear that?' type stuff, but you can pick up some amazing bargains. I got a cashmere Nicole Farhi coat for £120 – it would have been at least £700 retail. As usual, it's best for beanpoles, but they do stock bigger sizes. The first day (Friday) is best, but they do get new stock in throughout the weekend.

💬 Ann

STAY

I'm going to a ball in Heddon Street (W1) at the end of August and rather than traipsing back up to Watford at some God-awful time in the morning I am considering getting a hotel room. I am going off to university in October, which means two things:

1) I'm generally broke, so nowhere that breaks the bank

2) Since we are going our separate ways, this will be the last summer with my girlfriend and, to make it a night to remember I'd like to take her to a nice hotel, and am willing to pay some (but not loads, see above).

So basically, I'm looking for a nice hotel in central London (can be a taxi ride away) that is, if possible, a bit different and romantic and not stupid money. Oh, and somewhere that will do a real breakfast, no hot plates of pig's anus sausages and scrambled egg you could build a house with.

Anyone got any suggestions?

💬 Angus Prune

My sister stayed at Edward Lear's house a year or two ago (www.edlear.com). She said it was very reasonable, friendly, clean and a little bit funky, if not totally luxurious. It also has a nice history to it and she said she would definitely stay there again.

💬 Ella

Try www.wolseylodges.com. These are like upmarket B&Bs, but more like you are a guest rather than just £s. Some amazing houses round the country, but not stupid money and proper breakfasts. I'd like to keep it secret really, but seeing as it's a special occasion...

💬 Mr Ben

The best place I know to go to find cheap but acceptable accommodation in London is www.londontown.com. They've always got hotel offers on there – I got my parents a stay in a hotel with something like 60% off. Good luck.

💬 **Declan**

My husband and I just had the most incredible weekend at *Miller's Residence* in Notting Hill and I cannot recommend it highly enough. It's not youth-hostel-cheap but neither is it sell-your-kidney-expensive. Note – If you like modern minimalist chic then this is not the place for you. It is crammed, and I mean crammed, with antiques, memorabilia, Victoriana – you see something new every time you go into the salon/lounge or walk through the place and in your room. I have never encountered such a chilled, comfortable, charming and friendly hotel.

It was my 30th birthday and we requested a bottle of champagne – which we received at no charge. There are bowls with mountains of candy and chocolate throughout the hotel and in your room, and there is a free bar (yes, that says 'free') for all the guests to use. We opted to stay in the hotel when we weren't out at dinner just to enjoy the surroundings in the guest lounge. Breakfast starts at 8am and was still out at midday (when we got up and went downstairs) and not an eyebrow was raised. It would be the most memorable anniversary for you – and the Byron Room has a four-poster bed. Check it out at www.millersuk.com and book through Lastminute.com where they have deals.

💬 **Jodie**

SPACE

I've got a very talented artist friend who is in need of cheap studio space which will allow her to work as an artist three days a week while earning money elsewhere on the other two days to fund herself. She needs to find a studio in west/central London and it needs to be cheap! Without a studio, her painting will take a back seat and she's so good, I really want to help her find somewhere. Any suggestions?

Lindy

Try looking on the website www.artshole.co.uk (in their own words 'Specialising in Student and Independent Artists') which is a great resource for all arty things – studio space, current exhibitions, life models, work experience opportunities, courses, etc.

Bealos

And finally

HAIR

Can anyone help the man in my life find a sympathetic hairdresser? He has very long Goth hair, but as he is no longer a student, sees that this may be a problem when getting a job (except in Sci-Fi bookshops and Camden, obviously). Where can he go where they won't just go for the usual short bedhead look, but will try to achieve a haircut with personality that is still acceptable to employers? Or is this not going to happen?

💬 **Spikky**

Try Kenna at *Toni & Guy* on Kensington Church Street. He's a very good stylist and recently put forward for British Hairdresser of the Year. He'll cost you £40 but it will be worth it, trust me!

💬 **Kevin**

My boyfriend was a proud undercut owner until this time last year. After much deliberation, he came to my usual hairdressers to get it cut simply because they are more used to cutting off long hair and making it short and styled. It worked really well, despite him nearly crying when she chopped it, of course. So I would recommend that course of action.

💬 **Gilesy**

For a decent haircut try *Tusk* in Camden (very near Camden Underground) and ask for Conrad. He seems to be one of the more popular stylists so you sometimes need to book a bit in advance. He devised a cut and colour for me that's a bit different but I can still get away with working as a vet without getting funny looks from the clients. He's also really good when you have no idea what you want and will spend a bit of time coming up with suggestions for styles that will suit you. Definitely the best hairdresser I've had in a few years (and there have been many)!

💬 **C Fi**

Spikky, my friend Louise runs a lovely little salon called *Sessions on* Theberton Street, off Upper Street (near the *Screen on the Green*). She'll sit down with your bloke and chat with him about what needs doing, and they also keep a record of what cut he has for future reference in case he gets a different stylist next time round.

💬 **SFULG**

For haircuts that are cool, but not over the top, I always go to guy called Tristan (previously of *Fish* and *John Freida*) in Middlesex Street (Liverpool Street tube). The salon is called *HIMI* and it's right at the very end of aforementioned street, so you begin to feel like turning around as you're walking along it ,but don't as you'll be right on it by that point. He's actually the hair stylist from *Queer Eye for the Straight Guy* (UK) but don't let this put you off!

💬 **peelit**

TATTOO

Does anyone know of a good tattooist in London?

🗨 **Ed**

Ed, if you're looking for an excellent tattooist, I recommend *Tribalize*. I got a tattoo there eighteen months ago. Superb service and an excellent tattoo at a great price. The address is: 30 Lower Marsh, London SE1 7RG. Telephone: 020 7928 1231.

🗨 **Un-named**

Try *Into You* in St John Street, Clerkenwell. This is apparently one of the best in the whole of the UK. I had my tattoo done there, really professional, great designs and the staff are very helpful and kind (considering how much pain they're inflicting on you!).

🗨 **Gemma**

I had my tattoo done at *Original Skin* in White Hart Lane, North London. Excellent service and happy to do originals. Had a look through their books while waiting and they have some fantastic stuff of their own too.

🗨 **Milehigh**

PLUCK

Like most ladies I like to keep my legs, underarms and, ahem, bits, smooth and hair-free. Recently though I have grown weary of the amount of time and effort involved in shaving every day and have decided to go the whole hog and get rid of it once and for all.

A Google search revealed a plethora of clinics offering laser hair removal treatment but most seem like the kind of places you see featured on those 'When Cosmetic Treatments Go Wrong' shows you see on the telly. Can anyone that has had this treatment recommend a clinic that won't leave me with permanent scarring?

💬 **peaches**

I've had great success at *Bare Necessity* near Liverpool Street Station. Tanya and Kelly are great but all the girls there are good. Tel: 020 7247 0500.

💬 **KangaRue**

I can highly recommend Maureen Gillanders epilight system (www.epilight.co.uk). I think her London clinic is still some-where along Oxford Street. The really nice treatment ladies are fast and efficient. I wouldn't say the process was pain-free - I'd put it on a par with burning paper cuts. But you'll have to dig deep into your pockets for the privilege.

My underarms took four treatments, a few weeks apart, at £220 a go. But I didn't want to mess around with anything cheap, and the wonderful, permanent results have certainly been worth it.

💬 **Smoothy**

Peaches, have you thought about having aculight rather than laser? I had a course of treatment at the beauty salon in *Holmes Place* gym in the *Plaza* on Oxford Street. It's a bit bizarre – you have to wear goggles while they apply a sort of laser gun to where the sun doesn't shine (if you're having your, er, bits done) - but after just two treatments it was bikini line heaven. I would and have recommended it to everyone.

It's fab! Unless of course big hairy minges come back into fashion in which case you'd be in trouble because it is permanent.

💬 **bad girl bubby**

Peaches, for laser hair removal (and a wide variety of other treatments) I recommend *Bio Farm* in Lambs Conduit Street, WC1. It's a small and very professional clinic with good facilities, staffed mainly by Brazilians (for some reason).

I've been thoroughly satisfied with the treatments I've had there. And their prices are good too. That said, laser hair removal is an expensive exercise whichever way you look at it. But it will leave your skin smooth and, um, peachy.

💬 **GreyArea**

The Big Question

If you could give one piece of advice to someone moving to London for the first time, what would it be?

Mutilate the cover of your *A–Z* so you don't look so much like a disorientated newcomer, and instead look more like the cool kid at school with the graffitied folder. Be careful, however, that the contents remain legible, and that you choose band logos carefully.

💬 **Amelia**

Don't fall asleep on the tube on the way home after a night out.

💬 **Tim**

Walk 100 yards north from Oxford Street on a Saturday afternoon and see how quiet and lovely it is.

💬 **Ben**

When you're feeling overwhelmed, over-charged, over-exhausted and thoroughly sick of the place, just stop for a minute, take a deep breath and look up and around you – London is one of the most exciting and beautiful places in the world and you're living here. This never fails to make me feel proud to be a Londoner.

💬 **AP**

Don't rely on *LOOT* to find your first house-share. *LOOT* is full of freaks. Try something like www.flatshare.co.uk or www.moveflat.co.uk, where the rooms don't go within one day, and there are generally more normal, savvy people on there.

💬 **Gizzard**

Be proud of being in love with London. If you like it say so. Don't feel you have to join in with the moans about the tube and the weather and the volume of people and the tourists just because that's what Londoners do. Real Londoners stay here because we love it. Rubbish trains, expensive beer and busy streets etc., are what makes London what it is. Of the millions of people that live here each one has their own unique combination of favourite pub, shop hangout etc., and you'll find yours too. Saying London is the greatest city in the world isn't always cool but it's always true.

💬 **The Assassin Prince**

Buy a Travelcard. Then use it. A lot.

💬 **David**

Put the milk in *before* you put the hot water in (i.e. the same time as your teabag). London water is so skanky that bits float on top of your tea. Milk first stops this happening. This was the only tip given to me when I moved down and it has stood me in good stead for several years.

💬 **Lala**

Be open-minded. Do not expect London to be like anywhere else you've ever lived, and judge it on its own merits. Love it for what it is, not for what you wanted/expected it to be. And then you should be happy.

💬 **Caroline**

Live near to a good night bus service. I spent two years in Raynes Park after having lived in Belsize Park and all I remember about living there was the number of hours spent crawling through Clapham and Wandsworth to get home after missing the last train.

💬 **Jase**

Walk everywhere. Despite the hype, London is smaller than you think and it's a great way to get your bearings.

💬 **Liz**

Get a bus pass and get using those buses! You'll discover more about London than you ever would using the tube, you'll meet interesting people, see parts of the capital you never knew existed and get a wealth of dinner party stories. You'll be richer, better read, less stressed (man wasn't meant to be underground, it's not natural or right!) and you'll never be afraid to visit all those funny places like Hackney, Camberwell, Peckham, Crouch End etc., (collectively known as 'whatdoyoumeanyou'renotonthetube?')

Go on, be brave – set yourself free from the tyranny of the tube!

🗩 **Hannah**

Cycle/jog/walk around Clapham Common on a Sunday morning. It will open your eyes to just how diverse London can be.

🗩 **Marc**

Keep to the right on the escalators.

🗩 **Dave C**

Don't panic. It's not as big as you think it is, it's more of a series of villages/towns. Find a local bar and a local shop and you are on the way to feeling at home.

🗩 **Sarah**

The best thing I found out about London after years of living here is how pleasant and easy shopping in the centre of town on a Sunday can be... if you drive into town.

Depends on where you live, obviously. I'm near Westbourne Park, but I find I can drive to near Oxford Circus in about 15 minutes, park on a yellow line somewhere near Cavendish Square (behind *John Lewis* on Oxford Street) for free for as long as I want, stroll up and down Oxford and Regent Street, shopping for Britain then dropping stuff in the car as needed. Then there's no need to try and lug it all back again on the tube. It's brilliant. Make no mistake, London's traffic sucks but if you choose when and where to go carefully, owning a car really make life pleasurable even in this city.

💬 JC

Buy an *A–Z* and walk everywhere. If you're in zone one, try walking – you'll find loads of new bars, museums and restaurants. It won't take you much longer than the tube and it's a great way to feel at home in the place really quickly.

💬 Ben

Don't spend all your time with friends from Uni, School etc. ,– there are so many people to meet in London – some of them are crazy, but many of them are great. Oh, and it's going to take about a year before you say 'I really must visit/do more of the million things in London that I haven't got round to', at least two years before you actually start doing them and only then will you really appreciate the city for all it offers.

💬 Ben R

Living in London is generally expensive with extortionate rent and high taxes on anything fun. Make sure you have saved up enough money to live comfortably for a month before you arrive (this includes a month's rent, then double that to include deposit and then add living expenses). Pick up a copy of *LOOT* if you're looking for somewhere to live and don't want to pay estate agents' fees.

💬 Ferga

Stand in the middle of the carriage on a busy commuter train. If you stand by the doors, you'll be squashed for the whole journey and shoved every stop.

🗨 Carrot

Walk around. You see so much more of the city on foot, than on the tube, and you get a far better idea of where things are geographically in comparison to other places. Plus, you're far more likely to wander off down a side street and discover some great bar/restaurant/view that you would never have found without it – and then you can feel truly smug!

🗨 robram

Always use a traditional London taxi – a black cab – they will not rip you off and they are safe. *Never* use an unlicensed mini-cab and compromise your own personal safety for a few quid savings.

🗨 Nancy

Get a bike. Otherwise traffic or public transport will drive you insane.

🗨 Neil

Don't go out in the West End. It's everything you left your home town to avoid.

🗨 Dirty Sue

Take the riverboat from Westminster to Hampton Court to see some historic sights, how the other side live, and that there are some beautiful green places to visit.

🗨 Pippa

Buy a large fold-out *A–Z* map and stick it on your wall. It'll help you get your bearings a hell of a lot quicker than the tube map or using a map book with every district on a different page.

💬 **Tim1882**

I would think that regardless of how great an area is, or how nice the house you find is, your life can very quickly turn into hell if you haven't considered your commute. In central London all modes of transport have their pros and cons. If you are brave enough, however, and unless you are lucky enough to live on a direct tube line to work, then I would recommend a scooter. Was excellent for getting around, easy to park, and you also get to know London really well. Two things to be careful of are

1) London drivers are idiots; and
2) scooters are easily stolen.

Get a heavy lock and attach it to something immoveable whenever possible. I had a wheel clamp type thing, but they just lifted it into a van and drove off. Bastards.

💬 **Ramon**

Re-appraise your concept of time. In London it's not unusual to find your journey home takes almost an hour when meeting people. For someone who grew up in Kent, this would be a big expedition. In London it's normal.

💬 **Dom**

Don't move to Clapham, it is over expensive and overrated – go down the road to Balham or look east.

💬 **Emma**

Take buses everywhere for the first month. If you only ever use the tube you'll never really know how London fits together, the tube map gives such a distorted impression of the jigsaw. Take the bus – any bus – and just look out the window to see where it goes. You'll see things that you'd never otherwise see; remember streets and land marks; see bars and restaurants you'd like to try out; see great architecture and little hidden gems and realise just how close things are to each other. In fact *always* take the bus; it's cheaper, less crowded and much more pleasant.

💬 **Amanda**

Go to tourist attractions. Don't avoid them because you think you'll get around to visiting them eventually or because it's somehow uncool to mix with the tourists. Tourist attractions generally become such for a good reason: they're interesting.

💬 **General Joy**

If you get nothing else get yourself a small and up to date *A–Z* (A5 is best for fitting in a bag but with more detail than the pocket one). I have been living in London as a grown up for the last ten years and still find it indispensable to confirm vague directions such as 'just opposite that road near the old Tower Records on Piccadilly' or finding my way when diverted by roadworks or replacement bus services.

💬 **Stuart**

When walking down crowded and touristy streets such as Oxford Street, if you walk along looking at the pavement in front of you then other pedestrians subconsciously notice that you're not looking where you're going and will tend to avoid you. Makes for a more pleasant walk as you will not be bumped into by so many other people. Try it, it works.

💬 **Steve**

If you only go to one museum make it John Soane's House. If you want high street shops, go to Wimbledon's *Centre Court* shopping centre. It's literally right next to the tube and is never busy – a much more pleasant experience than Oxford Street.

💬 **Greta**

My advice for anyone new to London is to do a trip on one of those open-top tourist buses after you've been here for a few weeks. I know it sounds a bit naff, but on a bus you'll realise the disparity between navigating around London by tube map as most people do, and the geographical reality. From the bus you can see that Embankment is only down the road from Charing Cross, that tube station's are only minutes apart in the centre of town and you get a damn fine view of a beautiful city. If you bump into someone you know, behave like a Londoner and say you're showing some mates round.

💬 **Mod**

On a sunny day, go to the park at Crystal Palace for the afternoon. There are model dinosaurs which were constructed in the Victorian era. When the area went out of fashion they were left to rot, but recently restored they are now on display to the public once again. It's a peculiar experience; sitting reading the paper with a T-Rex on the horizon.

💬 **Alison**

Find a friendly face as soon as possible, even if it's only the local newsagent. Until you meet anyone, it looks like the unfriendliest place on earth.

💬 **Tim**

Give it time. It takes months, if not years to really get rid of that overwhelmingly frightened and unsettled feeling but once you do, you can really start to enjoy all the amazing things this frustrating, smelly, overcrowded but ultimately wonderful, city has to offer.

💬 Julie

Do not go out drinking in Leicester Square or around Piccadilly as the bars are over priced and full of tourists. Go to Angel or Old Street, a short tube ride away, where you get a good variety of bars and pubs that are frequented more by locals than by visitors.

💬 Kate

London isn't an eighth as big as you think it is. Especially the bit that you think is the biggest. Use the weekend to walk around London. That's when you see the best part of London, meet the most interesting people and learn that when the tubes inevitably break down or are rammed you can still get to work.

💬 Bobbers

When travelling around London, do not assume that place names that are nearly the same are necessarily nearby. For example, Finsbury Circus is nowhere near Finsbury Park and neither one of them is near Finsbury.

💬 Johnny T

Borough Market. On a Saturday/Sunday. Marvellous. See if you can accumulate enough free samples to constitute an entire meal. Then have a look at where they filmed *Lock Stock*.

💬 daveyt

Keep up! Nothing will brand you a tourist/provincial/undesirable as quickly as dawdling on the pavement, standing on the wrong side of the Underground escalators or stopping dead in the middle of the street to read the signs. Stride confidently and keep a pocket sized London *A–Z* to hand to help with tricky navigation. You'll be swanning around the capital like a native in no time!

🗩 **Mrs. Mooncat**

Avoid Piccadilly Circus, it's like Piccadilly Circus round there.

🗩 **David**

Forget about how expensive it is, don't panic about getting mugged/hit by an angry bus driver/ripped off at a bar, don't listen when people tell you it is a big scary place. Just have fun and enjoy London for the great city it is. If you don't mope around like a scared little puppy you won't get treated like one.

🗩 **TK**

When your heart goes out to a beggar in the cold and wet, resolve to give regular donations to a homeless charity to really help these people, rather than making a cheap guilt-avoidance donation, of which a high percentage will be spent directly on drugs (the percentage is apparently 85% in Lambeth). Help make a difference not a noose.

🗩 **do good-er**

Try and organise your first flatshare with the maximum number of people. Yes, there's a greater chance that you'll fall out with someone, but if there are around half a dozen of you that won't matter as much as if you fell out with your one mate. And if you've come straight from university, you'll probably be used to the communal lifestyle.

The advantages are that the burden of flathunting is shared
more bearably, and the weekly cost per room will probably
be under a hundred quid, which is the stuff of dreams
for most London flatsharers.

All the costs are divided (say) six ways, so that you can
afford to splash out on the odd luxury like a home cinema
system or a dishwasher. Utility charges and repair bills
or other unexpected costs aren't so scary. And if one person
moves out it won't cause a financial catastrophe.

Oh, and for flathunting, get the *AA London Street Atlas*,
because it shows most blocks of flats, and the others don't.

💬 **Russ**

Carry wet wipes with you at all times. Things, especially
anything that stands permanently outside, are filthy and you
will have black soot-like gunge on your fingers and in your
nose and ears within minutes if you don't regularly clean.

💬 **Jimmyjames**

Find out about the area you might live in. I never bothered
and ended up living in Docklands initially, which was bolx.
Could have been Hackney, Peckam or New Cross so I should
be thankful really. I now live in Greenwich and absolutely
love it. So, find out about London before you come: If you
want a busy, hectic, lively place maybe Camden, Brixton or
Clapham is for you. If you want a bit more quiet then
Putney, Hampstead (bit pricey) or Greenwich perhaps.
If you want to be nervous walking from the station to your
house then Hackney, Eltham or Tower Hamlets is for you.
My girlfriend lived in Bermondsey on her own for a year
and said it was rougher than ten bears.

💬 **Jez**

Don't expect anywhere, particularly food vendors, to be open on 1 January. Even in London. I've almost starved on many New Year's Days.

💬 **Commonplace Gent**

Don't do your first day's travel in rush hour.

💬 **Kathryn**

Set one day aside and just go up to a central London destination such as St. James Park, or Green Park, without a map, and just wander about, especially beyond the parks, down the side streets. You will discover lots, without the hassle of trying to see everything and it will be more exciting. Write down roads and landmarks and then cross-check them against a map when you get home. You will be amazed what you have covered.

💬 **Mon**

Check out the cheap factory outlets and nice cafés in Muswell Hill, North London. It's not on the tube and it feels like a little village in the middle of the big city!

💬 **Mariam**

The best piece of advice I was given when I moved to London was, find out about everything you should see, from the very naff, to the historic, and then do it all in a week. Once you've moved to London, it becomes so much a part of who you are, that you won't notice it anymore and sometimes that can be a real shame.

💬 **mourillio**

One piece of advice I'd give to anyone moving to London is never, ever, under any circumstances renew your travel card on a Monday morning. That is unless of course you have a thing for queues.

💬 **Rob**

Catch buses or walk as much as you can, instead of using the tube, until you know your way around. And look around as you travel. Its easy to get around on foot in London, and very rewarding, but you'll end up catching the tube from Leicester Square to Covent Garden unless you take my advice. And all us Londoners will then laugh at you condescendingly as you get on and off.

💬 **Dr Z**

Don't let the fear of crime put you off coming to London. A little common sense goes a long way in any city you visit. Be sensible, be confident and then relax and enjoy one of the greatest places on the planet!

💬 **Sarah**

I always want to tell people coming from outside London that just because Londoners don't chat away to strangers on the tube, it doesn't mean they are all horrid and unfriendly. The fact is that sometimes pretending other people aren't there when you have your nose in their armpit is the only way to stay sane. And for many people, a tube journey can be the only bit of their day when they don't have either a boss, or customers, or kids screaming at them for attention. Maybe we're not all rude – maybe we are just trying to retain a bit of peace and a bit of dignity!

💬 **Moocher**

If you're renting a house or flat, get one with a six-month contract (maximum), or one that allows you to leave without penalties before six months. Odds are that you won't like the first place you move to, and you don't want to be stuck there for a year.

🗨 **Will**

You haven't lived if you haven't been to Camden Market on a weekend.

🗨 **Sudonim**

Get cabs. Everywhere. The reason why celebrities from abroad love London is because they have chauffeurs. Without them London is torture. Parking anywhere you might actually want to go is impossible even for world class *Tetris* players, public transport will require you to exchange body fluids with the sort of people you have only previously seen in documentaries, and traversing London on a flimsy two-wheeled vehicle is hotly rumoured to be David Blaine's next stunt. The black cab is the instant, zero-fixed-cost chauffeur for anyone not listed in *Vanity Fair*'s New Establishment. When you look at it that way, it's really not that expensive. And when you look at London swinging past you through the windows of your warm, dry, private, yet cheap limo, you'll know it's worth it. Without black cabs London is torture. With them, it's possibly the most glamorous city in the world. At least, it is until you get out.

🗨 **Carlotta**

Explore.

🗨 **Dominic**

Never, ever eat at an *Angus Steak House*.

💬 **Salty**

Join London by London (www.londonbylondon.co.uk).
We'll look after you.

💬 **LondonByLondon**

Acknowledgements

Thanks to:

Abi, Adam Fergus, Al, Albert, Alex, Ali, Alison, Alleged rhythmless boyfriend, Also Anonymous, Amanda, Amelia, Andrew, Andy H, Andyandy, Ang, Angus Prune, Annie, AP, Annie Mole, Anonymous singleton, Ant, Aquagirl, ArPF, Atheist, Atobagofan, ATP, auawsha, Aunt Flo, Avid Fan, B-), Babyangel, bad girl bubby, Bankgirl, Barmaid, Batfink, Bealos, BeeG, Bel, Ben, Ben R, Benners, Bib, Big Sis, BikerBoz, Billy, Billy Gee, Billy the Kid, BillyGoat, BiologyMan, Blade Maestro, Blakey, Bobbers, Bobbuilder, bookemdanno, Boy, Brad Finley, braindead geordie, Breakfastfiend, Briony, Bryan Fadders, Bus Guru, C Fi, Camelpoo, Carlotta, Caroline, Carrie B, Carrot, Cassius, caterpillardriller, cdouble, Charl, Charlie, chaz b, Chells, Chris, Christophe, Chz, Cinders, Cinders4, CJ, Clairey, Clefty, ClubManager, cocktail gal, Commonplace Gent, Conehead, Costumekitten, Crazy Eddy, Crouch Ender, Curly Wurly, Curmudgeon, Daddio, Damian, Dan, Dave, Dave C, daveski, Davey, Daveyt, David, Deborah, DebsfromN1, Declan, Dirtos, Dirty Sue, Disgruntledworseoffbiker, Dixon, Do good-er, Dom, Dominic, Dr Bone, Drew, Drinker, Dr Z, DT, Dumb Brunette, dwp, Ed, Eddie, Eggplant, El Capitan, El Presidente platinumdan, Ella, Em, Emma, F, Feebs, Fineart, Fishface, Fishy Lips, Flameboy, Flapper, Flash Bobby, Flatpack, Fred, Frederick, Friendly Geek, Fulcanelli, Furydoll, G, Gail, Galatea, Garth, Gavin, Gemma, General Joy, Gentleman Loner, Gil, Gilesy, Giz, Gizbourn, Gizzard, Goldenanorak, GoldenEyes, goldsoundz, Gorilla, Gradvalax, Granty, GrayArea, Greta, Greg, Gromski, Growler, Gruncher, Hannah, Harri, Haunted by Keane, Heed, Hels, Hiccup, Hong Kong, House Mouse, Hun, Hungry Jim, Iain, Ian, Ianem, Ils, Integer Spin, Jack, Jacquelyn, Jamella, James, James W, Jase, JazzMag, JC, Jean, Jeff's Vodka & Soda, jen greengo, Jenn, Jess, Jez, Jezter, Jif, Jimmy H, Jimmyjames, Jo, Jodie, Joe, John, John-James, Jon, Jonny, Jonny T, Joseph T, Josh, Judetheobvious, juicy, Julie, Julio, K, Kaffkins, Kaiser, KangaRue, Katanajim, Kate, Katherine, Kathryn, Katkin, Katkins, KB, Kenning Tom, Kenton, Kev, Kevin, Kirstie, Kite, Kitty, kljazz, KT, Lady Barnes, Lala, Lalalondon, Laurence, Leia, Leytonstone, Linda, Linda Palermo, Lindy, Lisa, Little G, Little Gem, Little Lady B, little miss, Little Miss B, Lillibet, littlejon, Liz, LizardPUB, Liz-beth, llama, loaf, Lolly, Lolo, longjon, Looska, Lou Ling, Luc, Luke, Lulabelle, LuLu, Madpickle, Magpie, Mandy, mappeal, Mariam, Mario, Marc, Mark, Martinez, Matthew, Matthew, Sqweno, Maureen, Maxbiker, Maybeitisallinmyhead, McTeague, Meg, Michael, Mickey D, Mike, Milehigh, Miles, Mills, Missing London, Miss Lake, Mister Bob Dobelina, Mistress, Mod, Mon ,Monkavich, Moocher, Mourillio, Mouse, Mr and Mrs Smith, Mr Ben, Mrs Mooncat, Mudge, Mudgewah, Naeonlite, Nancy, Nancy Drew, Natasha, nb, Neil, Neil LeM, Neuman, Nic, Niceday, Nick, Nick Nack, Nick Nocks, Nick the Greek, Ninja Angel, No, I Don't Need You To Hold My Willy While I Pee, No Pikeys, Orac, Originalpubgirl, Oz, Pasty, Patrick, Lizzie, Paul, peaches, pedal power, PeeGee, Peelit, Peggy, Pesk, pesk, Pete, Phatflaresblack, Piggywigs, Pinksquid, Pippa, Plugus Maximus, Pockettiger, Pol, Polly, Prenders, Pretty Polly, Pretzel, prguru, pubster, pussinboots, Rachel, Rachie, radar, Raffles, Rastaban, Ray, RC, Rich, Rich Rich, Richard, Richsaint, Rob, Robram, Roger roger, Rombo, Ruby ru, Russ, Sachin, Salty, Sarah, Sarong, Scally, Scintillate, Scottie Scottie, serene, Sergeant Matron, SFULG, Shelleuk, Simon Stacpoole, Sinsita, SJW, Sladey, slayer73, Sleepy Tim, Small Fi, Smalldelapaul, Smoothy, Snooker loopy, snow, Snowbeetle, Sophie, Spammed, Spaniel, SparkleT, Sparky, Spikky, Steve, Stocky, strangeciara, Stu, Stuart, Sudonim, Suey, Superflake, Suzanne, Suzy, Tallchap, Ted, The Assassin Prince, The Horse, The Jungle Warrior, The Secret Person, thefaris, Thepnut, ThPhphThphh, Tiddle, Tiddler, Tiddles, Tigger, Tikki, Tim, Tim 1882, Timotheus, Tizzy, TK, Tom, Tonytone, Trev, Tris2000, trombonegirl, Tube Guru ,Tubeworm, Vero, Voet, W, Weak Serve, Will, William, Willlis, Wireless Hooligan, Xpablo, Zed, zeroGravitas, Zoe, Zoz.

Finally, we would like to thank Leigh Jones and his team at Staziker Jones (www.stazikerjones.co.uk) who designed and packaged this book. Without Leigh's advice and support, not to mention his unwavering belief that we might one day be able to pay him something, this book would never have existed. Thank you.

Places to visit

Places not to visit